Jalal al-Din Rumi (1207-73 CE) was born in Vakhsh, in the northeast of greater Persia. A disciple of the Sufi tradition, he was the figurehead of the Whirling Dervishes. Prolific as both a poet and religious teacher, his poetry is what he is best remembered for: the *Masnavi*, a narrative poem of 25,000 verses in six volumes, is widely considered to be the greatest literary spiritual masterpiece ever written.

Franklin D. Lewis is Associate Professor in the Department of Near Eastern Languages and Civilizations at the University of Chicago. He is a specialist in Persian literature and the author of the bestselling biography, *Rumi: Past Present, East and West*, also published by Oneworld.

RELATED TITLES

Rumi: Past and Present, East and West
Franklin D. Lewis

Rumi: A Spiritual Treasury
Compiled by Juliet Mabey

Rumi: Swallowing the Sun

Poems Translated from the Persian

Franklin D. Lewis

ONEWORLD

A Oneworld Book

First published in Great Britain and the Commonwealth
by Oneworld Publications, 2008

This edition published in 2013
Reprinted, 2013, 2020

ISBN 978-1-85168-971-2
Ebook ISBN 978-1-78074-120-8

Typeset by Jayvee, Trivandrum, India
Printed and bound in Great Britain by Clays Ltd, Elcograf S.p.A.

Oneworld Publications
10 Bloomsbury Street
London WC1B 3SR
England

TABLE OF CONTENTS

ACKNOWLEDGEMENTS

Many individuals have helped me puzzle out complex passages in the new poems of this collection, particularly Naeem Nabili-Akbar and Heshmat Moayyad, to whom my deepest gratitude. My colleagues John Woods, Robert Dankoff, Kagan Arik, Tahera Qutbuddin and John Perry have also kindly put their expertise at my disposal in response to specific queries. I am especially grateful to readers and reviewers of my earlier study, *Rumi: Past and Present, East and West* (Oneworld, 2000) who have provided useful comments and correctives about the translations contained in that book, which have been incorporated here. Though there have been many, Hassan Lahouti and Ibrahim Gamard stand out. For their encouragement, I am indebted to many further friends and colleagues, including Soheila Amirsoleimani, Carl Ernst, Saeed Ghahremani, Hasan Javadi, Gökalp Kamil, Manuchehr Kasheff, Todd Lawson, Sunil Sharma and Ehsan Yarshater. For the opportunity to work on further translations and to think carefully and critically through many poems, I am thankful to the graduate students at the University of Chicago who studied Rumi with me, including Samad Alavi, Rajeev Kinra, Hajnalka Kovacs, Mary Musolini and Azad Amin Sadr. Thanks also to Katayoun Goudarzi, on whose 2006 CD *Rooz o Shab* several translations first appeared. A very big thank you to the very patient people at Oneworld, especially Juliet Mabey, Kate Kirkpatrick, Mike Harpley and Novin Doostdar. More patient still, Foruzan, Sahar and Ava, who continually put up with lexicons and *Divân*s strewn across living room, den and divan, with scattered papers, distracted thoughts and stolen moments – they have my apologies, my undying gratitude and my love.

Franklin Lewis, Chicago

INTRODUCTION

ON TRANSLATING PERSIAN POETRY

The extraordinary success and influence of certain translations and adaptations of Persian poetry into western languages – those by Sir William Jones, Wolfgang von Goethe, Friedrich Rückert, August von Platen, Ralph Waldo Emerson, Edward FitzGerald, Basil Bunting, Robert Bly, Coleman Barks and Dick Davis – makes the burden of the translation past and present especially weighty. A meta-translation question must therefore be resolved in the mind of any would-be Persian translator before they begin: who is the intended audience of this translation, and what use do they have for it? One may of course translate for the love of translating, but even then the endeavor may run aground on unforeseen shoals. As Ḥafeẓ (d. 1391) famously observed in the first line of the first poem of his Collected Poems, or *Divân*, a line whose first hemistich is in Arabic and the second in Persian:

alâ yâ ayyohâ s-sâqi ader ka'san va nâvel-hâ
ke 'eshq âsân nemud avval vali oftâd moshkel-hâ

Come, Saqi, pour out a cup and pass it around;
Love – which first seemed easy – comes fraught with complications

That word "Saqi" (*sâqi*) was introduced to many an English-speaking reader in 1868, in the phrase "the Eternal Sákí," which appeared in the second edition of Edward FitzGerald's translation of the *Rubáiyát of Omar Khayyám*. FitzGerald published four different editions of his Khayyám translation; in the first edition of 1859, the word "Sákí" had not appeared – though Goethe and others had previously introduced it to western languages in their translations and adaptations of "Eastern" poetry. But with the passage of time FitzGerald seemed to increasingly feel the English use of the word "Sákí" appropriate: he introduced it in 1868 (quatrain # 47, which became # 46 in subsequent editions) and then added a second occurrence of the word for the third and fourth editions (1872 and 1879, respectively) of his *Rubáiyát* in a rather prominent place in the poem: an apostrophe to the Sákí in the first line of the final quatrain. FitzGerald's *Rubáiyát* was one of the most, indeed perhaps the most, successful of verse translations ever made into English, so our "Sákí" (or *Sâqi*, according to a more contemporary transliteration) was often seen in English in the last decades of the nineteenth through the middle of the twentieth century, especially after Omar Khayyam societies became active in most of the English-speaking capitals. The Scottish short-story writer H.H. Munro (1870–1916) even chose Saki as his pen name, so we might assume that it is well attested in English lexicons. And yet, the *Oxford English Dictionary* gives no entry for "saki" in this meaning, only for the homonym that describes a particular genus of South American monkey (to which definition the *Merriam-Webster* dictionaries merely add that "saki" can also be a variant spelling of the Japanese potation, sake).

As for those readers familiar with the meaning of "saki/saqi" derived from translations of Persian poetry, they may be uncomfortable with the overtones this adapted English term has subsequently acquired. "Saki/saqi" may now inadvertently evoke an orientalized presentation of Omar Khayyam and the "East" which was once prevalent in popular Western culture, but is now about as believable and fashionable as the harems depicted in Hollywood films of the silent era through the 1940s. That is to say, "saki" may strongly remind us that the Romantic and post-Romantic translators of Persian held some assumptions we can no longer readily share, and may evoke a colonialist western attitude that modern translators would like to avoid. A change in orthography from *sákí* to *sâqi* may be seen as cosmetic, not enough to distance our stance from that of the nineteenth century.

In an effort to avoid retrograde associations, we may be moved to substitute our own preferred term for the person or profession intended by *sâqi*, namely the one who tends to and serves the wine at a drinking party (a *majles-e sharâb*, or Persian wine symposium). As a literary ideal, this saqi is rather androgynous: attractive, young and supple, bright-complexioned and smooth-skinned in body and face (if facial hair is present at the temples, along the jawline or above the lip, it should be soft and downy). The imbiber hopes the saqi – an obscure object of desire at times depicted as a boy, at others a girl, perhaps a Christian, or a Zoroastrian – will be generous and liberal, too. A modern translator may seek a different term to conjure up these memes of the ideal saqi. Depending on the type of establishment one frequents, the kind of poetry and party one favors, the musical genres one prefers, or the gender one desires, one might consider Ganymede, Libationer, Sommelier, Wine-steward, Skinker, Pot-boy, Waitress, Server, Bartender, Barista... Of course, none of these terms comes free of its own cultural baggage. Although this noun "saqi" is an important part of the semiotic universe of Persian poetry, we may despair of finding an equivalent, and therefore avoid naming it altogether by means of some locution, such as a direct address: "Come, fill the Cup!"

TRANSLATING RUMI

There may not be a Rumi society or club in every English-speaking metropolis, but Rumi has many devotees, and Coleman Barks' renderings have captured the public imagination almost as much as did FitzGerald's rendering of Khayyám. Rumi is generally considered the most outstanding representative of mystical poetry in the Persian tradition, and he has indeed been called more than once the world's greatest mystic poet (an oddly competitive and hierarchical notion, which, despite the irony, does signal the stature and reputation of the poet).

Rumi was born in 1207 of the Common Era (604 A.H. by the calendar he would have used), most probably in the town of Vaxsh. He lived in Transoxiana, including Samarqand, before his father emigrated for political and professional reasons, probably around 1216, taking the family to Syria and Anatolia. Eventually they settled in Konya, the capital of the western Seljuq dynasty, where Persian literature was patronized, and where Rumi lived from 1229 until his death in 1273, with the exception of several years spent studying Islamic law and theology in the colleges (*madrasa*s) of Aleppo and Damascus in the 1230s, after his father's death.

"Rumi" is in fact only a toponymic, meaning a man who lived in "Rum," or Rome, referring to Christendom generally, but more especially Byzantium, as a political domain. Geographically speaking, at least from the perspective of northwest Persian and the Levant, this meant Asia Minor, or Anatolia, which was in Rumi's day the center of the Seljuq empire, but nevertheless still a region on the periphery of Islamdom. As one might imagine, many medieval Muslim figures living in Anatolia were also called Rumi ("the Greek" or "the Anatolian"), and indeed, until more recently, Rumi was not familiarly known this way in the West. Instead, he was known as Jalál al-Dín Balkhí (Jalâl al-Din Balkhi), a man who had reputedly emigrated from Balkh, before arriving in Rum. Rumi's disciples, however, used the Arabo-Persian title "My Master" (Mowlavi), or "Our Master" (Mowlânâ) to address him. This latter form, Mowlânâ, is how the Persians typically speak of him today, though it has become somewhat more familiar to westerners in its Turkish pronunciation, as Mevlana.

In America it has been repeatedly stated in the press, in library journals and even in academic articles that Rumi is the best-selling poet in America. Insofar as high school and college classes continue to teach the traditional canon of Shakespeare's sonnets, or Walt Whitman, Emily Dickinson and T.S. Eliot, this seems rather incredible. I have not seen comparative publishers' documentation for the sales figures of the various poets, but UNESCO's Index Translationum, which inventories some 1.6 million translations made since the 1970s in scores of the world's languages, lists Shakespeare as the only major poet among the top 50 translated authors of any language in the world.[1] While far more translations were made from English than from any other source language, English ranked only fourth as a target language for translations in 2006 – more works were translated into German, Spanish and French than into English, and translations

---

[1] These statistics were taken at the end of 2006 from the Index Translationum website: http://databases.unesco.org/xtrans/stat/xTransStat.a?VL1=A&top=50&lg=0. The database, which is as yet incomplete and contains significant lacunae, is nevertheless a useful starting place. Disney Productions as composite author, Agatha Christie, Jules Verne, Vladimir Lenin and the children's author Enid Blyton come, in that order, ahead of Shakespeare. By 2013 Edgar Allen Poe, Rudyard Kipling and Goethe had also entered the top 50.

into English were only slightly more numerous than translations into Japanese, Dutch and Portuguese. Indeed, citing a consultant for Bowker, which tracks the publishing business, a *New York Times* article announced in 2006 that

> American publishers have one of the lowest translation rates in the Western world ... Only 3 percent of books published in the United States are translations (4,114 in 2005) ... compared with, for example, 27 percent in Italy. As a result, linguists contend, much of the English-speaking world knows little of other countries and cultures.[2]

By way of comparison, Persian ranked twenty-fifth as a target language, with translations into Persian just notches above the number of titles translated into Turkish and Arabic.[3] But to comparatively evaluate the extent to which Rumi is being translated, one would need to consider the number of works for which Persian is the source language of the translation. According to these statistics, the number of works translated from Persian is comparatively meager, ranking in thirty-fourth place, behind translations from Latin (in eighth place) and from pre-modern Greek (up to the conquest of Constantinople in 1453) in eleventh, and behind translations from Arabic (16th), Hebrew (20th), Sanskrit (26th) and Serbian (33rd).[4] UNESCO's 2006 data clearly stands in need of continued compilation and collation, but nevertheless provides a useful index, indicating that in terms of the total number of titles translated from Persian into all other languages, Omar Khayyam (199) still stands ahead of Rumi (170), even though Rumi has more titles published in English (44) than does Khayyam (30).[5] Of course, none of this actually settles the

---

[2] Dinita Smith, "Found in Translation: Endangered Languages," *New York Times*, 21 April 2006, Late Edition – Final, Section E, 31, 4.
[3] See http://databases.unesco.org/xtrans/stat/xTransStat.a?VL1=L&top=50&lg=0, though one suspects that the statistics fail to notice many translations into Persian, since Iran has experienced an incredible explosion of translated titles published in the last two decades.
[4] http://databases.unesco.org/xtrans/stat/xTransStat.a?VL1=SL&top=50&lg=0
[5] Rounding out the top five most translated Persian authors, in descending order, we find Nezâmi, Baha'u'llah and Hâfez, according to UNESCO's data. http://databases.unesco.org/xtrans/stat/xTransStat.a?VL1=A&top=10&sl=PES&lg=0

question of which poet (Khayyam, Rumi, Whitman, Eliot, Ginsberg, Bly, Angelou?) sells the most books in America.

Nevertheless, English poems with the name of Rumi as author have certainly sold in amazing numbers, in both print and audio formats. More than a dozen translators and para-translators (versioners, adapters and impersonators) have published English renderings of Rumi, and many of them remain in print and on bookstore shelves. Versions by established poets like Coleman Barks, Robert Bly and W. S. Merwin; others by Nevit Ergin, Kabir Helminski and Jonathan Star; some directly from Persian by Nader Khalili, John Moyne and Shahram Shiva; and many others beside, have created and fed an unprecedented interest in the poems of Mowlânâ Jalâl al-Din Rumi. Robert Bly and Coleman Barks obviously demonstrated a remarkable vision and foresight in bringing this particular poet to wider attention. Of course, a fair number of Persianists had already produced translations, and continue to do so, directly from the original language of Rumi – among them, A.J. Arberry, J.C. Bürgel, William Chittick, Abdulbaki Gölpınarlı, Talat Halman, Jawid Mojaddedi, Reynold Nicholson and Annemarie Schimmel. Some of their efforts are very literary in their own right. And even those that are not intended to be read as poetry in English have not only helped us understand the meaning of difficult or ambiguous passages, and the significance of various images and allusions, but have also provided cribs for the popularizing poets who do not themselves know Persian, from which to chisel out poems in contemporary American idiom. As a result of all these efforts, at the very least it does seem quite safe to say that Rumi is currently the world's best-selling thirteenth-century poet (especially if we allow that Dante did not compose his *Divine Comedy* until the fourteenth century).

PERSIAN LITERARY ADAPTATION TO ENGLISH

For a Persianist, all this translating, versioning and adapting must be good news, right? But our growing awareness in recent decades, due to the theorizing of the orientalist and post-colonial gaze, has taught us to suspect subconscious epistemological biases and motivations in our encounters – both intellectual and political – with the non-western world, most especially with the Islamicate world, Robert Irwin's *Dangerous Knowledge: Orientalism and Its Discontents* (Woodstock, NY: Overlook Press, 2006) makes a vigorous attempt to rehabilitate the reputation of that "motley crew of intellectuals and eccentrics who brought an understanding of the Islamic world to the west," most of whom had been tarred by the brush of Edward Said's seminal work *Orientalism* (New York: Pantheon, 1978). Said himself later argued that it is literature – representations of lived experience, rather than the explanations of political or religious abstractions – that can dispel the "ideological fogs" in which the western gaze has obscured the Middle East, especially in the post-9/11 atmosphere, now that the mass media and the internet have given us a heightened sense of being informed about the Middle East.[6]

One might then harbor a positive view in general of the translators, very few of whom had consciously nefarious intentions, and yet still worry about the meta-meaning of translation. As Julie Meisami puts it in her review of the history of translations of Hafez, who died a little more than a century after Rumi:

> There are many reasons for translating a work or works from one literary tradition into the language of another. Only rarely is the impulse purely aesthetic; more often, the aesthetic motive (if there is one) is overshadowed by other, ideological motives which, spoken or unspoken, determine to a great extent the practical approach taken. Translation is never a simple act of transference, but involves complex questions of authority: the authority of the text and of its author, of patrons and publishers, of the translator (whose expertise is assumed), of the receiving culture, and, perhaps most important, the authority of [quoting Andre Lefevere:] "the image a translation creates of its original author, its author, its literature, its culture."[7]

Generally, it would seem that translations of Rumi in the era famously described as a "clash of civilizations" are being put to ecumenical uses with which peaceful and tolerant people ought readily to agree: to demonstrate

---

[6] Edward Said, "Impossible Histories: Why the Many Islams Cannot Be Simplified," *Harper's Magazine*, July 2002, 69–74, at 74.

[7] Julie Meisami, "Hafiz in English: Translation and Authority," *Edebiyat*, 6, 1995, 55–79, p. 55.

the depth and vitality of Islamic traditions of spirituality, to inspire the vast unchurched population in the West with inspiration for a new age of spirituality, and even for constructive political purposes. As an example of the latter, we might recall the 15 March 2000 issue of the *New York Times*, where a group of Iranians published a full-page advertisement with a line of Persian poetry in calligraphic Persian script, ascribed to Rumi, along with an English rendering by Coleman Barks. The text of that advertisement verse read: "Out beyond ideas of right doing and wrong doing, there is a field, I'll meet you there." If the wording seems clumsy and uncommunicative, the purpose was made clear by the small text below it:

> 70% of the current population of Iran was nine years old or younger when the Americans were taken hostage in 1979. On February 18th, in a democratic election, the citizens of Iran voted for reform. Shall we meet them in the field?

Of course, this kind of message poetry comes with an expiration date, and with the defeat of the Iranian reformists in subsequent elections, it may now seem rather stale. But in any case, it is certainly startling to see the use of medieval poetry to urge negotiation, when modern quotation from medieval texts has sometimes had the opposite effect of condemning another religion or political tradition.

The realization that this process of viewing or translating the other is subject to distortions and ideologies invisible to the onlooker is, of course, not so entirely new: in the 1930s Samuel Chew was already observing, albeit in a less abstract way, that in the Elizabethan era English visitors to the "Orient" carried with themselves "a quantity of superstitions, fabulous lore, and old wives' tales" as part of their baggage, and after arriving there they were generally "more desirous to have it confirmed than to put it to the test" of actual observation.[8] Some of these pre-impressions had already been formed by the depiction of Persian manners and costumes on the English stage, as well as John Mandeville's mendacious travel account,

---

[8] Samuel Clagget Chew, *The Crescent and the Rose: Islam and England during the Renaissance* (New York: Oxford, 1937), 542. See also Hasan Javadi, *Persian Literary Influence on English Literature* (Costa Mesa, CA: Mazda, 2005), 18. Javadi's study has greatly informed the present essay.

though the effects of that were somewhat mitigated by two or three reports of later Elizabethan travelers who actually did visit Persia in person.

An early mention of Persian poetry, and the presentation of what may be a kind of second- or third-hand English translation, appears in Puttenham's (whether George, or his brother Richard, has been disputed) work *The Arte of English Poesie* (1589), where four pattern poems in "translation" were said to have been "bestowed" on Puttenham in Italy by a longtime sojourner "at the courts of the great Princes of China and Tartarie."[9] It is difficult to tell if these are actual translations, or imitations, and indeed the eighteenth century's vogue for the Oriental Tale would lead to the publication of several works questionably introduced as translations, and attributed to authors otherwise obscure to us, whose authority nevertheless stemmed from their putative oriental origins. Antoine Galland's *Les mille et une nuits* (Paris: Barbin, 1704–17) (The Thousand and One Nights) was translated to English more often than Rumi, most often not from Arabic, but from Galland's French. The first anonymous translation, the so-called "Grub Street edition," appeared as *The Arabian Nights Entertainment* (London: Bell), beginning in 1706. Hot on its heels came François Pétis de la Croix' *Thousand and One Days, or the Persian Tales*, rapidly translated to English in 1714 two years after its original French publication as *Les milles et un jours, contes persans.* Pétis de la Croix purportedly translated this from a book authored or compiled by a certain "Dervis Moclès," chief of the Sufis in Isfahan, with whom de la Croix had studied Rumi's *Masnavi* (a book de la Croix had found theological and difficult), but no original Persian manuscript has ever been found. The tales of *A Thousand and One Days* seem to be taken from different sources, perhaps including the imagination of de la Croix himself, who, at the very least, must have re-shaped the tales into their present form, even though he really did meet and receive help in compiling Turkish and Persian stories from this "Sincere Dervish"

---

[9] George Puttenham, *The Art of English Poesie*, ed. Gladys D. Willcock and Alica Walker (Cambridge: Cambridge University Press, 1936), 91–5. Cited in Javadi, *Persian Literary Influence*, 25.

(Darvish Mokhleş) in 1675.[10] Other famous Persian characters, authors or tales in European literature are, however, acknowledged to be partially or wholly fictive, including Montesquieu's Persian letter-writers, Usbeck and Rica, and Sir James Morier's Hajji Baba of Isfahan.

By 1742, it was already possible for William Collins to publish a *Persian Eclogue*, which he pretended to be written by a poet from Tauris – i.e. Tabriz – who had died of distemper but wrote, probably, in "the beginning of Sha Sultan Hosseyn's Reign" (sic). In this work Collins found a way out of the neo-classical Arcadia into a warmer style, the "rich and figurative" style of the Arabians and Persians, which he characterized as follows:

> There is an elegancy and wildness of thought which recommends all their compositions; and our genius's are as much too cold for the entertainment of such sentiments, as our climate is for their fruits and spices. If any of these beauties are to be found in the following ECLOGUES, I hope my reader will consider them as an argument of their being original. I received them at the hands of a merchant, who had made it his business to enrich himself with the learning, as well as the silks and carpets of the PER-SIANS. The little information I could gather concerning their author, was, that his name was ABDALLAH, and that he was a native of Tauris.[11]

---

[10] *Les Mille et un jours. Contes Persans, traduits en Français par Pétis de Lacroix*, 5 vols. (Paris, 1710–12). Much later, a new edition was published in a single volume (Paris: August Desrez, 1840). For a study of this text, see Franz Hahn, *François Pétis de La Croix et ses Milles et Un Jours* (Amsterdam/New York: Rodopi, 2002), and also the memoir of Pétis de la Croix in *Relations de Dourry Effendi ambasadeur de la porte othomane auprès du roi de Perse. Traduite du turk et suivie de l'Extrait des Voyages de Pétis de la Croix rédigé par lui même* (Paris: Ferra, 1810). De la Croix says he acquired a manuscript called "Hezaryek-Rouz" from Dervis Moclès in Isfahan in 1675; no such volume survives, and if such a text actually served as the basis for his *Thousand and One Days*, it would appear to have consisted of a redaction in Turkish of a Persian retelling of the Arabic text *Faraj ba'd al-shidda* (Hahn, pp. 45–53). An Ottoman Turkish translation of de la Croix' French *Thousand and One Days* was published in 1290 A.H./1873 as *Alf ün-nehar ve nehar*, the stories identified as having originally been Indian in origin; the relation between this work and the earlier Turkish redaction of *Faraj ba'd al-shidda*, namely the *Muhayyelât-i ledün-ü ilâhî* of 'Ali 'Aziz Effendi of Crete (written c. 1211 A.H./1796–7 and published in 1268 A.H./1852–3), is discussed in Andreas Tietze, "'Azīz Efendis Muhayyelât," *Oriens*, 31 December 1948, 248–329, esp. pp. 252–4.

[11] *Oriental Eclogues, Written Originally for the Entertainment of the Ladies of Tauris, and Now Translated* (London: J. Payne, 1757), vi–vii.

Collins goes on to say that "the works of Orientals contain many peculiarities, and that, through defect of language, few European translators can do them justice."[12]

But Oliver Goldsmith, in his *The Beauties of English Poetry* (1767), thought Collins' effort "very pretty," even if "the images, it must be owned, are not very local." Goldsmith presciently suggested that "the description of Asiatic magnificence and manners is a subject as yet unattempted among us, and I believe capable of furnishing a great variety of poetical imagery."[13] In his own *Oriental Eclogues* of 1782, John Scott is aware of Collins' prior effort, but perhaps more inspired by the "ingenious" Sir William Jones' "elegant translations and imitations of Eastern Poetry," especially his translations of Hafez. Scott's address to Jones is testament to the truth of Goldsmith's prediction:

> The Asian Muse, a Stranger fair!
> Becomes at length Britannia's care;
> And HAFIZ' lays, and SADI's strains
> Resound along our Thames's plains.[14]

At least a score of book-length collections of Hafez in translation were published in English in the eighteenth and nineteenth centuries, and in Germany, poets and composers were also caught up in the vogue. Even so, it is generally accepted that Hafez has yet to find an entirely satisfactory English translator, though many would-be poets have climbed into print on the back of his reputation. Elizabeth Daryush, daughter of Robert Bridges, published her first book of poems as *Sonnets from Hafez and Other Verses* (London/New York: H. Milford/Oxford University Press, 1921), containing four translations of Hafez and fifty poems of her own. More recently, Daniel Ladinsky, also innocent of a knowledge of Persian, has done two or three books with the name "Hafiz" on the cover,[15]

---

[12] Collins, *Oriental Eclogues*, viii.

[13] Oliver Goldsmith, ed. *The Beauties of English Poesy*, 2 vols. (London: William Griffin, 1767), 1:239.

[14] John Scott, *The Poetical Works of John Scott Esq.* (London: J. Buckland, 1782), 332.

[15] *I Heard God Laughing: Poems of Hope and Joy: Renderings of Hafiz* (New York: Sufism Reoriented, 1996 and New York: Penguin Books, 2006); *The Subject Tonight Is Love: 60 Wild and Sweet Poems of Hafiz* (North Myrtle Beach, SC: Pumpkin House Press, 1996; and

some of which present poems of his own, inspired by Hafez (or more accurately, inspired by the iconic notion of Hafez as a mystic poet), and others of which rely on the nineteenth-century translations of H. Wilberforce Clarke, who did know Persian. The same has been true for Rumi – poems have appeared "in praise of Rumi" (1989) by an anonymous author (apparently Lee Lozowick, edited by Regina Sara Ryan), or as *The Love Poems of Rumi* (1998), consisting of four re-printed Rumi poems by Coleman Barks, among many other poems said to be, not "direct" translations, but "moods captured" from Rumi.

By the time of John Scott's observation, the efforts of that "ingenious" Sir William Jones, member of Dr. Johnson's famous circle, had already started a vogue for learning Persian and specifically for translating Hafez. "Oriental" Jones' translation of "A Persian Song of Hafiz," based on a famous ghazal of the poet (*agar ân tork-e shirâzi be dast ârad del-e mâ râ*), had indelibly characterized the form of the Persian ghazal as "orient pearls at random strung," a phrase that – minus the qualifier "orient" – aptly describes how most Persian rhetoricians had indeed conceived the structure of the ghazal, when they bothered to talk about it:

> Go boldly forth, my simple lay,
> Whose accents flow with artless ease,
> Like orient pearls at random strung :
> Thy notes are sweet, the damsels say ;
> But O! far sweeter, if they please
> The nymph for whom these notes are sung.[16]

This aesthetic assumption about the Persian ghazal has tended to inform the critical understanding, not to mention the practice, of translators in English, and to some extent in other languages of the West. Indeed, though this theory of "disunity" in the ghazal was vigorously challenged from the 1940s, it still has its contemporary proponents among both

New York: Penguin Compass, 2003); *The Gift: Poems by the Great Sufi Master* (New York, Arkana, 1999).

[16] Sir William Jones, *Poems, Consisting Chiefly of Translations from the Asiatick Languages, to which Are Added Two Essays*, 2nd ed. (London: W. Bowyer and J. Nichols, 1777), 63.

critics and translators, especially for the Urdu ghazal. The astounding thing about all this was that the phrase "orient pearls at random strung" appears nowhere in the Persian text of Hafez' poem, but was a deliberate interpretive interpolation of Jones, who was merely doing what he and many other eighteenth-century translators assumed one should do to nativize a foreign work in English. The poem first appeared in his *Grammar of the Persian Language* (London: W. & J. Richardson, 1771), a book that so delighted its readers that modern language pedagogues would do well to investigate its methodological secrets; Edward FitzGerald reports spending many delightful hours with it and longing to return to it on those occasions when he was compelled to tear himself away. Of course, in those days, a serious gentleman or lady would often attempt to learn a foreign language so as to better appreciate its poetry (to say nothing of attempting to translate it). Jones' project, as made explicit in his 1772 collection *Poems Consisting Chiefly of Translations*, was to reinvigorate English poetry by recommending "to the new world a species of literature which abounds with so many new expressions, new Images and new inventions." His "Essay on the Poetry of the Eastern Nations" elaborated:

> If the principal writings of the Asiaticks, which are reposited in our pub-lick libraries, were printed with the usual advantage of notes and illustra-tions, and if the language of the Eastern nations were studied in our places of education, where every other branch of useful knowledge is taught to perfection, a new and ample field would be open for speculation; we should have a more extensive insight into the history of the human mind, we should be furnished with a new set of images and similitudes, and a number of excellent compositions would be brought to light, which future scholars might explain, and future poets might imitate.[17]

It is not inconceivable that some of Jones' reasoning here, if not his pre-cise wording, could still have been advanced two centuries later as one of the rationales for the creation of the Area Studies Centers funded by the

---

[17] Jones, *Poems, Consisting Chiefly of Translations*, 189–90.

U.S. Department of Education – at least until Martin Kramer's *Ivory Towers on Sand: The Failure of Middle Eastern Studies in America* (Washington: Washington Institute for Near East Policy, 2001) attacked the Middle East Centers for not producing useful knowledge, such as a prior prediction of the attacks of 9/11.

With respect to translation, as Meisami has pointed out, Jones here exemplifies the first of Susan Bassnett's "two conflicting tendencies" in nineteenth-century translation: that which "exalts translation as a category of thought, with the translator seen as a creative genius in his own right, in touch with the genius of his original and enriching the literature and the language into which he is translating." The tendency opposed to this, as Bassnett describes it, "sees translation in terms of the more mechanical function of 'making known' a text or author."[18] It would seem that with the popular explosion of interest in Rumi in the past twenty-five years neither category exactly applies; translation as a category of thought is far removed from consideration, insofar as most of the commercially successful "translators" do not work from the languages in which Rumi wrote (principally Persian, with some Arabic), but from cribs found in old scholarly translations, or with native-speaker aficionados who do know the language of Rumi, or some other language (such as Turkish) to which Rumi has been previously translated.

PROSODY AND FORM

In the present work two basic forms of poetry are translated, one narrative and one lyric. The narrative poetry occurs mostly in the Persian couplet form, from Rumi's magnum opus, the *Masnavi-ye ma'navi* ("The Spiritual Couplets" or "Couplets of True Meaning"). This work presents problems for the translator, to be sure, but they are, I think, somewhat more tractable than the problems presented by Rumi's lyrical poems. This is in no small part because of the incredibly extensive commentary tradition on the *Masnavi*, which has for centuries been glossed and explicated,

---

[18] Meisami, "Hafiz in English," 56–7, citing Susan Bassnet-McGuire, *Translation Studies* (London: Methuen, 1980), 65–6.

with whole volumes being dedicated to just the eighteen opening lines of the 25,500-plus-line *Masnavi*. Reynold Nicholson has also provided us with a full, explanatory translation of *The Mathnawí of Jalálu'ddín Rúmí* (London: Luzac, 1925–40), and more recently, Jawid Mojaddedi has undertaken a rhymed verse translation, of which the first of the six books of the *Masnavi* has appeared.[19]

Numerous other collections of excerpts from the *Masnavi* exist in translation, both by poets and by scholars, such as A.J. Arberry's *Tales from the Masnavi* and *More Tales from the Masnavi* (London: George Allen & Unwin, 1961 and 1963), but these tend to extract the tales from the larger context of the morals that are drawn from them. This is not the proper way to read the poem, though it is a habit born of the great length of this work, and perhaps also reinforced by the three-hundred-year-old habit of reading the tales of the Thousand and One Nights cycle in bits and pieces. The collection you presently hold in hand is not an effort to translate the entire *Masnavi*; instead, it contains passages from the *Masnavi* which are necessarily excerpted from their larger context, torn from the soil in which they thrive, like the reed torn from its bed in the opening of the poem. A few of the translations included here provide the entire narrative portion of a tale, but many others are short excerpts that do not tell a story. The only excuse I can offer for this procedure is the desire to illustrate and highlight certain voices, categories and ideas in Rumi's poetry; but the poem best rewards a through-reading from start to end.

It is worth noting that all passages of Rumi's *Masnavi* follow the same meter, namely *Ramal maḥẕuf*, which is based upon sextameter lines,

---

[19] *The Masnavi, Book One*, tr. Jawid Mojaddedi (Oxford/New York: Oxford University Press, 2004) – this work won the Lois Roth Prize for Literary Translation from Persian. There were also previous efforts besides Nicholson's (which appeared in eight volumes from 1925 to 1940 along with his critical edition and notes to the Persian text) to translate the *Masnavi*. Sometimes this took abridged form, as in the case of E.H. Whinfield's effort (London: Trubner, 1887), which is still in print; sometimes it took the form of single books of the six-book *Masnavi*, as in the efforts of Sir James Redhouse for Book 1 (London: Trubner, 1881) and Charles Edward Wilson for Book 2 (London: Probsthain, 1910); and sometimes as single stories, or excerpted passages and selections.

consisting of two equal half-lines, and composed of a repeating quantitative foot [long – short – long – long], which is, however, curtailed by one syllable just before the caesura and again at the end of the line [long – short – long], as follows: ¯ ˘ ¯   ¯ ˘ ¯   ¯ ˘ | ¯ ˘ ¯   ¯ ˘ ¯   ¯ ˘ ||. In the couplet form, the rhyme occurs just before the caesura (|), and at the end of each line, which is more often than not end-stopped, though enjambment is permissible. The rhyme changes from one line to the next: a | a || b | b || c | c|| and so on, but the English translations of the *Masnavi* passages in the present collection do not rhyme. Rather, they are presented variously in free verse, blank verse or other syllable-count forms.

The lyrical poems, in contrast, come from Rumi's *Divân-e kabir* (Great Divân), also known as *Ghazaliyât-e Shams*, "the Ghazals of Shams," in whose voice many of the poems are spoken, or to whom many are addressed. Rumi's Divan contains some 3,200 ghazals plus other lyrical forms (quatrains, strophic ghazals and odes). In contrast to the *Masnavi*, comparatively little has been written about the ghazals as poems, and there is no comprehensive commentary or critical analysis.[20] This is a particular problem, it seems to me, because the ghazal cannot be translated well without an operative notion of how this form functions structurally, what it seeks to do and what its horizon of expectations is.

---

[20] In English, the books of William Chittick, *The Sufi Path of Love: The Spiritual Teachings of Rumi* (Albany: State University of New York Press, 1983); Ali Dashti, *A Voyage through Divan-e Shams*, tr. Sayeh Dashti (Tehran: Ketâbsarâ, 2003); Fatemeh Keshavarz, *Reading Mystical Lyric: The Case of Jalal Al-din Rumi*, 2nd ed. (Columbia: University of South Carolina Press, 2005) and Annemarie Schimmel *The Triumphal Sun*, 2nd ed. (Albany: State University of New York Press, 1993) are all quite useful. To these may be added the articles by Amin Banani, "Rumi the Poet," and J. Cristoph Bürgel, "'Speech Is a Ship and Meaning the Sea': Some Formal Aspects of the Ghazal Poetry of Rumi," both in *Poetry and Mysticism In Islam. Levi Della Vida Symposia*, ed. A. Banani, R. Hovannisian and G. Sabagh (Cambridge: Cambridge University Press, 1994), as well as the articles by Wojciech Skalmowski in *Studies in Iranian Linguistics and Philology* (Cracow: Wydawnictwo Uniwersytetu Jagiellońskiego, 2004) and J.C. Bürgel's "Ecstasy and Order: Two Structural Principles in the Ghazal Poetry of Jalāl al-Dīn Rumi," in *The Legacy of Mediaeval Persian Sufism*, ed. Leonard Lewisohn (London/New York: Khaniqahi Nimatullahi, 1992): 61–74. Although there are a few works in Persian that treat the poetics of the ghazals, surprisingly little has been done in this regard, given the towering stature of Rumi and the popularity of his poems. A scholarly commentary of Rumi's *Divân* would be an especially useful project.

And yet, the ghazal may no longer be in need of introduction, as it has established itself not only in the English lexicon (along with other borrowed poetic terms, like "terza rima"), but has also increasingly become a living part of our poetic repertoire. There are now entire anthologies of English-language ghazals, and several well-known American poets have practiced the form. Indeed, for the centenary of the passing of the Urdu and Persian poet Ghalib (Ghâleb) in 1969, Aijaz Ahmad assembled a notable workshop of contemporary American poets (W.S. Merwin, Adrienne Rich, William Stafford and Mark Strand, inter alia) to work, courtesy of the Asia Society, on free verse translations of Ghalib's Urdu ghazals.[21]

The contemporary nativized English ghazal is, then, refracted through a modernist lens – with a particularly South Asian model in mind, wherein the Urdu ghazal is the dominant inspirational model. Though the Urdu ghazal ultimately derives its inspiration from the versification, ethos and motifs of the classical Persian form of the ghazal, it nevertheless took shape, like the Ottoman gazel, late in the history of the Persian form, and reflects stylistic assumptions arising well after the period of Rumi. In addition, the ghazal as practiced by recent English poets is naturally suffused with a post-modern ethos, and a different attitude toward verse structures. Thus, with some exceptions, the sense of the ghazal conveyed by modern poets in English is somewhat attenuated from the model that Rumi practiced.[22]

The Persian ghazal, and not the European sonnet, as has been claimed, may be one of the world's "oldest poetic form[s] still in wide popular use."[23]

[21] Aijaz Ahmad, ed. *Ghazals of Ghalib: Versions from the Urdu* (New York: Columbia University, 1971, reprinted New Delhi: Oxford University Press, 1995).

[22] A quite authentic Persian-style ghazal in English verse has been published by John Hollander as "Ghazals" in *The Nation*, 10 July 1989, p. 10.

[23] Paul Oppenheimer, *The Birth of the Modern Mind: Self, Consciousness, and the Invention of the Sonnet* (Oxford/New York: Oxford University Press, 1989), 3. There are older poetic forms, of course, in China, and the Arabic *qasīda* is older than the Persian ghazal; however, the Persian ghazal remains robustly alive and well, many poets having continued to practice the traditional form over the past half century (Rahi Mo'ayyeri, Akhavân-e Sâles, Feridun Moshiri, M.R. Shafi'i-Kadkani, Hushang Ebtehâj), and some even making it their form of choice (Shahriyâr, Simin Behbehâni).

It may also be one of the more conventional, at least for the period we are considering. The oft-repeated comparison of the sonnet and ghazal can be useful in that both are the premier fixed forms of lyric poetry in their respective traditions, but this juxtaposition also creates certain expectations and anxieties, and has had a tendency to draw us into the trap of Eurocentric assumptions.[24] In particular, the question of the architectonics of the ghazal, the how and why of the sequence of its motifs and ideas, can become convoluted by too much cross-comparison with the sonnet. Pursuit of the principles of organic unity in the ghazal has vexed western critics as much as it has informed their understanding, and in recent years some have disavowed any organizing principle in the ghazal other than prosodic conventions. Indeed, an anthology of English ghazals has been titled *Ravishing Disunities*, based upon the ghazal's critical reception as a form that is only unified at the level of the metrical line, with scant relation between the lines. The individual lines are held together in this view mostly by the glue of prosody: rhyme and meter, as well as refrain. Since the anglicized ghazal typically lacks the structure of rhyming verse, its cohesion is artificially achieved through secondary sound patterning and graphical organization of the lines on the page. *Ravishing Disunities* clues us to the fact that in the English ghazal form we do not, and should not, expect any evident linear progression or structural unity – indeed, perhaps the absence of a developed argument, in contrast to the sonnet, for example, is the anti-aesthetic that animates the English-language concept of the ghazal.[25]

Johann Wolfgang von Goethe found the Persian ghazal in 1814 through the Austrian Joseph von Hammer-Purgstall's (1744–1856) translation of the *Divân* of Hafez – or, more aptly, von Hammer-Purgstall's translation of Sudi's Turkish commentary on Hafez. Goethe thought the ghazal more comfortable than the sonnet, and made it a part of the program of what he would later call *Weltliteratur*. Goethe and

---

[24] Already in the eighteenth century Sir William Jones made the comparison between the ghazals of Hâfez and the sonnets of Petrarch, a comparison frequently repeated until recently, as for example in Reuben Levy, *An Introduction to Persian Literature* (New York/London: Columbia University Press, 1969), 33.

[25] Agha Shahid Ali, *Ravishing Disunities: Real Ghazals in English* (Hanover, NH: Wesleyan University Press of New England, 2000).

von Hammer-Purgstall inspired others, like Friedrich Rückert (1788-1866) and August von Platen (1796–1835) to write adaptations of Persian ghazals and original German "ghasels." From Germany the ghazal form – and the Persian poets who practiced it – came to the attention of Ralph Waldo Emerson and Henry David Thoreau, as well as Walt Whitman, not to mention a whole host of composers (Brahms, Schubert, etc.), who set innumerable translated ghazals as the text of lieder. Rückert, the first to provide a close parallel to the form in German, compared "Die Form des Ghasels" to ottava rima when he introduced the Persian ghazal, via his adaptations of the poems of Rumi:

> *Die neue Form, die ich zuerst in deinen Garten pflanze,*
> *O Deutschland, wird nicht übel stehn in deinem reichen Kranze.*
> *Nach meinem Vorgang mag sich nun mit Glück versuchen Mancher*
> *So gut im persischen Ghasel, wie sonst in welscher Stanze.*

> The new seed which I in your garden sow,
> O Germany, for your rich harvest wreath will grow;
> And thou who once ottave rime made
> Thy gifts now in ghazals of Persia show![26]

Going back to its Arabic origins, *ghazal* (or *taghazzul*) signified discourse about love, or talk with women (this from a male-centric point of view, of course). The Arabic genre of ghazal developed as a lyrical poem of indeterminate length on the topic of love. The Persian ghazal started out this way, but added several features to make it a fixed form. Persian and Arabic verse both follow a quantitative poetic metrics, and a given poem must observe the same meter throughout, as well as a mono-rhyme. Each line is divided metrically and graphically in two, usually with a syntactic break at the midpoint. The rhyme appears at the end of each line of the poem, but in the opening line of the ghazal the rhyme occurs twice, once at the end of the first hemistich and again at the end of the second hemistich,

---

[26] Hendrik Birus, "Goethe's Approximation of the Ghazal and its Consequences," in *Ghazal as World Literature 1: Transformations of a Literary Genre*, ed. Thomas Bauer and Angelika Neuwirth (Beirut: Ergon Verlag, 2005), 427. See also Hubert Tschersig, *Das Gasel in der deutschen Dichtung und das Gasel bei Platen* (Leipzig: Quelle & Meyer, 1907).

where the line comes to an end. Oftentimes, in addition to the rhyme, a Persian ghazal will also feature a refrain (*radif*) right after the rhyme, anything as short as a single-syllable word up to a multi-syllabic phrase. This of course adds a formal predictability at the end of each line, which may seem quite repetitious at first. However, the anticipatory contemplation of exactly how the poet will traverse this horizon of expectation, typically in a poem of between seven and fourteen lines in length, creates a certain suspense, and the potential to unfold an aesthetic surprise.

Finally, in the last line, or perhaps the penultimate line of the ghazal, the poet should call upon his authorial persona, or pen name, thus incorporating himself in an address as he exits from the poetic stage. The ghazal thus looks something like this, reading from left to right:

By the twelfth century, the Persian ghazal had developed from a topical genre into a fixed form observing the formal requirements outlined above, and as the ghazal became increasingly determined by form, it was liberated thematically from the concerns of romantic love. It became a vehicle for a variety of additional themes: didactic, mystical, political and artistic. The conventions of the genre assume an "I–Thou" dialogue in which the poet's persona – cast in the role of a (usually unrequited, or rarely requited) lover – addresses an absent, or a present, beloved, who is usually uncaring or even deliberately cruel. Alternately, the speaking persona might be a homiletic man of religion exhorting the backsliding faithful; or a mystical guide enlightening the initiates; or a subject praising the ruler; or a servant praising God.

The topoi and imagery of the ghazal are delimited and conventional. Poets were not expected to speak autobiographically, except in vague terms, though generation after generation of poets did manage to reveal uniquely individual styles within these conventions. The poet's pen name, representing a persona, interrupts the reverie that has been created in the body of the poem, allowing him to achieve an ironic distance from its pathos. Sometimes he will praise his own prowess as a wordsmith; at others he may pithily, often self-deprecatingly, encapsulate the mood of the poem in a phrase. In this line the poet may partially answer the dilemma that has been posed, or resign himself to suffering over the ineluctable workings of the universe, fate or love. He may call for wine, or for silence, in recognition that his dilemma is insoluble. In any case, with this apostrophe to his persona, the poet effectively signs his pen name (*takhallos*) to the tableau vivant he has created.

In the case of Rumi, the ghazals typically end with an invocation to or evocation of Shams-e Tabriz, his spiritual mentor, whose voice he internalized. Alternatively, Rumi may call for silence toward the end of the poem, as a realization of the ineffability of the experience he has been attempting to describe. Rumi speaks with many voices in his ghazals: the desperate voice of the lover destroyed by separation from the beloved, the importunate pleading of the disciple with his master, the praise of the lover of the beloved, the didactic tone of the master to his disciple, the awe of the worshipper before the *mysterium tremendum*, the wise sage who knows a way out of suffering or perplexity, the human being astounded by nature and the workings of the world, the celebrant of festivals and rites, the energetic singer who cannot repress the impromptu urge to versify the mundane things going on around him. He also manages to break down conventions of thought and poetry and language.

TRANSLATOR'S APOLOGY

Since the publication of *Rumi: Past and Present, East and West* (Oxford: Oneworld, 2000), several friends have suggested that the translations contained in that book be presented in a more accessible, stand-alone format, for use in the classroom, or for readers uninterested in the biography or reception history of the poet. While this idea appealed to me, given all the translations of Rumi that were already on the shelves of bookstores – and which continue to appear – it seemed an almost superfluous gesture. Rumi has become an icon of popular spirituality, if not quite of popular culture. Versions of his poems are recited to brides and grooms at weddings in North America, and UNESCO has declared 2007 as the year of Rumi, in commemoration of the eight-hundredth anniversary of the birth of the poet. Although British scholarship laid the groundwork for the current vogue for Rumi with translations of his poetry done directly from the Persian, his wider popular appeal began largely as a counter-culture phenomenon, tied up with developments in American poetry and spirituality. But the academy has taken notice, as well, and doctoral dissertations in theology and religion, or comparative literature, are now being written to compare Rumi with Meister Eckhart, St. Francis or Walt Whitman, among others. Unfortunately, Persian – the primary literary language of Iran, Afghanistan and Tajikistan, and the language in which Rumi composed the vast corpus of his poetry – does not today enjoy the central role it once did in foreign language study in the English-speaking world. There are relatively few Persian language programs in the universities of North America, so despite Persian's relatively uncomplicated grammatical structure, many of the poets, writers and scholars newly interested in Rumi cannot read him in the original.

Several collections of Rumi's poems done by "translators" who do not read the original language have generated phenomenonal response and reached a wide audience of English-language readers. But reliance upon second-hand versions, adaptations and impressions of the poems cannot suffice for serious academic study and comparison, or for those who genuinely look to Rumi as a spiritual guide. Versions of his poems crafted so as to make Rumi speak like a modern mystic for a modern audience, as if he were born in the United States in the twentieth century, may tend to give a solipsistic picture of his mental and religious universe, and reinforce our already iconic image of Rumi. We are comfortable with this iconic Rumi, a great saint and teacher whom we think we may have met before, since we carry around with us some vague preconceptions about how saints, Sufis, gurus and other wise teachers from the "East" behave, and the way they speak and how we should bow before them.

My aim in these translations, done from the original Persian and

Arabic, was not to nativize Rumi's poetry, or to omit what seemed foreign or unpolished. These translations seek to present Rumi in literary English, but in an idiom that does not elide his beliefs, erode his worldview, evert his style or excise lines that do not quite seem to achieve the desired effect. Of course, I hope to have presented Rumi in idiomatic (American) English, employing a theological and spiritual vocabulary that does not seem alien or awkward to modern readers who are not products of Rumi's tradition and training. However, rather than bringing Rumi's world to modern America, the emphasis has been to bring modern English to the world of Rumi. The premise has been that, if Rumi were to come somehow to our modern shores, he would speak, like many other immigrants who arrive as adults, with an "accent." These translations do not attempt to erase this accent, even when his images may occasionally feel strange, his locales disorienting, his ideas pre-modern or pre-secular, his allusions in need of explanation.

Rumi himself was an émigré from Central Asia who left his homeland as a child and eventually settled in Anatolia. It has been remarked that "the past is a foreign country," and in this respect, Rumi is more estranged from us than a modern immigrant. He lived in a cosmopolitan, multi-cultural environment, but one in which each person was identified, even by how they dressed and comported themselves, with a particular religious tradition. His own affiliation was unabashedly Islamic. Although he displays a largeness of heart and a remarkable empathy of understanding, his beliefs stem from his education in Islamic scripture and tradition, and his worldview stems from his mystical training and praxis. To Rumi, the universe is theo-semic. Perhaps this is one of the qualities that make him so appealing to modern readers – his mysticism is infused with a kind of natural theology that resonates with personal, experiential spirituality, and is not hidebound by dogmatic creeds and untested doctrines. His empathy for human frailties, his understanding of the sinner and the backslider, his tolerance for those of different faiths (including Jews, Christians and Zoroastrians), none of this should obscure the fact that his beliefs were not entirely harmonious with "new age" spirituality. Rumi did believe in the superiority of Islam and looked to various saints of the Islamic Sufi tradition as necessary guides to true spiritual progress.

Although Rumi's *Masnavi* has been repeatedly glossed and extensively studied and commented upon, the poetics of the *Masnavi* have not received extended attention and the poetics of his lyrical poems – his ghazals as literary artifacts and poetic constructs, rather than as expressions of his mystical teachings – remain relatively understudied. A handful of books and articles come to mind,[27] but much remains to be uncovered and understood. When the Hebrew Bible, the New Testament or the works of Dante, Chaucer or Shakespeare are translated into other languages, there is often a significant scholarly literature that helps translators explain particular cruxes or more creatively conceive the poems as structures and literary devices. Such studies will no doubt buttress the work of future translators of Rumi, but the existing translations and versions also provide a guide to thinking about the poems – what they mean, how they hold together and how they do or do not work in another language. Because the act of translation is itself often an instructive way to grapple with and gloss a poem, I hope that these renderings may contribute in some way to that process.

Free verse has been the most often preferred form to engage with Rumi's ghazals in English. The contrivances demanded by meter and rhyme inevitably result in the loss of precision (in comparison with Persian, English is rhyme-impoverished). In any case, relatively few contemporary readers seem to clamor for or expect traditional verse forms. As I began to work on translations of ghazals, my own models of emulation were Ezra Pound's *Personae*, and the imperative to "Make it New!" Though I have tried some experiments in meter and syllable count, in general I thought that the poetry would sound more sincere in free verse. I still generally believe this, despite what has been pointed out by Alistair Eliot in his essay "Translating Poetic Forms":

> Much has been said of the difficulty, unnaturalness, and even insincerity of "obeying" poetic conventions. Well, it is difficult and I suppose unnatural to ride a bicycle – at first. Maybe it would be more sincere to fall off.[28]

---

[27] See the works listed in note 20.
[28] *Translation and Literature*, v. 2 (Edinburgh: Edinburgh University Press, 1993), 68.

One might observe that the Persian ghazal being a highly conventional form, the effort to translate it into something that appears unconstrained and sincere is misguided, or simply misleading. But contrary to the impression created in the most often read English versions of Rumi, the aesthetic conventions that inform Rumi's ghazals include thick sonorities, dizzying cadences, repeated internal rhymes, and paronomasia. To capture some of this in English, free verse affords the best possibilities. Furthermore, despite a relatively simple grammatical surface, there is a complex theological depth and erudition behind much of the vocabulary of the poetry. Rumi's language often imparts to the ideal reader a significance that would take a short paragraph of notes to explain for the reader not versed in Sufi poetry or Islamic theology. In order to engage and highlight these aspects of the poetry and, one hopes, give them spirit in English, free verse seemed desirable. I have used the graphical arrangement of words on the page to try to bring out structural connections, as well as to illustrate phrasing.

Finally, this collection also affords me an opportunity to rethink some of the wordings, or to correct a few mistakes, in translations of Rumi I have published previously, and to add other poems which I have translated since then. They are here organized thematically in thirteen chapters, juxtaposed to highlight certain recurring ideas, motifs, genres and voices in Rumi's poems. Notes are provided where it was thought necessary to understand the poem. Transliteration has been kept as nonintrusive as possible, and should be self-explanatory for those who know the original languages. Because the Koran (*Qur'ān*) is not far from the surface in many of Rumi's poems, an effort has been made to signal quotations on the surface of the poem, by setting them in italics, and by giving verse numbers so that readers unfamiliar with the allusions may easily look them up.

I

ORISONS TO THE SUN:

Poems of

PRAISE AND INVOCATION

You are the light which told Moses
"I am God I am God I am God I am."

— from Ghazal 1526

Shams-e Tabriz, through your sun
we shine just like the moon.

— from Ghazal 1579

Sun of Truth and Faith, pride of Tabriz! Speak!
— but it is your voice that mouths all my words.

— from Ghazal 2056

My thoughts and reflections inspired by you —
As though I were your phrases and expression.

— from Ghazal 1683

SUDDEN RESURRECTION! Endless mercy!*
Blazing fire in the thickets of thought!
   Today you came laughing
      unlocking dungeons
      came to the meek
      like God's grace and bounty

You are antechamber to the sun
You are hope's prerequisite
You are sought
   seeker
   terminus
   principia
You pulse in every chest
   adorn every idea
   excite desires
then permit their realization
Spirit-spiring, irreplaceable
delight of action and cognition.

All the rest is pretext, fraud –
the former, illness; the latter, cure
We're jaundiced by that fraud
heart-set to slay an innocent
Drunk, now on *angel eyes*   [K44:54]
now on plain bread and soup
Taste this intoxication,
drop your ratiocination
savor these delectables
drop the debatables
a little bread and greens
should not entail so much trouble

* Ghazal 1

2

You implement a multichrome design
cast it like a net
white over Byzantium
black in Abyssinia
throwing them into war
concocting "a wonder never seen before"!

Box my spirit's ear in secret
dodge all others with excuses
Spirit shouts out "Lord release me!"
By God, my monarch, what a jest!

Silence!
I am so frenetic
I rushed from fray
   toward refuge by the battle standard

Put down the paper
Snap the pen
   The Saqi enters
   Cheers!

O MOUTHPIECE of God*
Eye of truth
Salvation of creatures from this seething ocean of fire!
How pre-eternal your mastery
How peerless your royalty!
deliverer of the soul
from attachment's travails

You swoop upon souls
walking the ways of sacrifice
all of them dying to know
whose soul is worthy to be game
For what creature can claim your love
when the Creator's glorious light
is in love with your beauty?

What remedy can you recommend
for me who am hunted down by love?
I'm racked in love's convulsions,
my physician with power to heal!
Your grace says approach
your wrath says withdraw
let me know which of the two to obey

O Sun of souls
O Day-star of truth from Tabriz
from each beam you radiate
a spirit emanates,
subtle
eloquent

* Ghazal 1310

LOOK AT that face*
   those manners
   that frame
   those cheeks
   those arms and legs
   That complexion
   that strength
   that shining orb
       filling out that shirt

Shall I compare to cypress? meadows?
   to tulips? jessamine?
   to the candle or the candelabra?
   or to the rose dancing in the breeze?

O Love lit like an agiary, assuming form and hue
Robbing the caravan of hearts along the highway
   Good sir! Give us some respite.

In flames and enflared I pass the night to dawn
How blessed my victory at *The Sun in the zenith*   [K93:1]
I spin around his bright orb
   greet him without lips
throw myself down to earth
   before he calls out "Come get it!"

Rose garden and paradise on earth you are
the eye and the light of the world you are
and also searing pain of the world
when your steps turn to cruelty
I come to pledge my life

* Ghazal 5

5

You say
    Don't bother me, go!
I bow and obey and withdraw
you say
    Come here, you fool!
His image joins company with fiery lovers
    May your face
    never for a moment
    leave our sight!

Heart, patience!
Why so distracted from your focus
Do you ever steal an hour of sleep,
of a morning? in the evening?
The heart replies
    His beauteous face
    those two bewitching narcissi
    his brow of hyacinth
        rubies sweet to taste

Love,
    everywhere blessed by fair name and good repute
last night I christened you anew:
        Pain Incurable

You,
the splendor of my being
the mover of my spheres
    send flour, my dear, as grist
        to stop the mill grinding to a halt and spinning loose

No more will I speak,
say this line and that's enough:
    My being melts in this desire
        Befriend us, Our God!

WHAT A BANNER, what a standard*: There is no God but God!*
    Planted on the pinnacle of pre-existence: There is no God but God!
How the King, like Moses, raises dust
from the sea of being and the void!   There is no God but God!
The quality of purity's
modeled on his humility
displayed in God's presence in pre-eternity: There is no God but God!
One wrong from him bests a billion rights
What wondrous, pleasant tyranny!   There is no God but God!
Every spot where he cast his glance
a million Eden-gardens grow   There is no God but God!

One fine day from sorrow's sea
I'll reach the shore
cast up by waves of grace and bounty   There is no God but God!
Any one you see sorrow's grip
has caught no scent
of spirit from my King   There is no God but God!
All eyes that refuse collyrium
from the King of Tabriz,
what wondrous loss and lamentation!   There is no God but God!

My heart and soul surge with the shout:
"*Are you not?*"
The King hears a thousand voices: Yes! There is no God but God!
The paradise of grace
the greatness of the prince
    Shams al-Din
What a wondrous cure of suffering: There is no God but God!

* Ghazal 2407

7

My heart circles
like an intimate
around Tabriz –   The sanctum sanctorum of There is no God but God!
How pleasant would it be for me to ask:
                    Who is it at the door?
and hear him say: It's me.   There is no God but God!

II

Poems of

FAITH AND OBSERVANCE

Flee to God's Koran

If you feel melancholy, longing for
a mi'râj *high above the wheel of life –*
The Arabian steed will take you there
It waits for you, in the field of fasting

A beast will never shine with learning's light –
Your body's beastly; don't let it stop fasting!

– from Ghazal 1602

My son, don't read Koran for outward sense!
A demon looks on man and just sees clay
The outward Koran is like man's body:
its features visible, its soul concealed
A man's own kith and kin may never know
his soul a hair's breadth in a hundred years

– *Masnavi* Book 3: 4247–9

Don't be more than others. So I urge my heart
Go be a salve of kindness – make no one sting
If you would have no other do you harm
Bite no back – do no bad deed – keep no bad thought
– Quatrain 993

Every prophet, every saint has his path
but as they return to God, all are one
– *Masnavi* Book 1: 3086

Love's folk live beyond religious borders
The community and creed of lovers: God
– *Masnavi* Book 2: 1770

Mind of the universe! Point of view
makes all the difference we see between
the believer, the Zoroast, the Jew
– *Masnavi* Book 3: 1258

The conflicts among men stem from names
Trace back the meaning and achieve accord
– *Masnavi* Book 2: 3680

FLEE TO God's Koran, take refuge in it;*
Merge there with the spirits of the prophets.
The book contains the acts of the prophets
those fish of the pure sea of Majesty.
If you read the Book without acceptance,
what profit in meeting saints and prophets?
When you accept the stories as you read,
the bird of your soul will feel encaged.
A bird imprisoned in the cage must seek
release, or failing that, is ignorant.
The only souls to have escaped the cage
are the prophets, mankind's befitting guides.
We hear them from beyond sing melodies
of faith: "Here is your path, this way release."
This is how we escape the confining cage
no recourse from this cage but by this path.

* From *Masnavi* Book 1: 1537–44

SWEEP ALL AWAY with the broom of "No"! Every king or prince has a*
herald for every ceremony. The herald which sweeps aside both worlds
from before the face of the Courtiers and Kings of Holiness is the phrase:

THERE IS NO GOD BUT GOD

> Everything keeps you distant from your quest
> whether words of blasphemy or of belief
> everything holds you back from the Friend
> whether images of beauty or of beast
> You'll clean no thorn and thistle from this path
> unless the creedal NO serves as your herald
> When NO casts you from fame into confusion
> Then follow Godhead's light through BUT to GOD

* From Rumi's *Seven Sermons*

THE MOTHER of fasting*
comes to her children
bearing gifts
Don't let slip your hold
my child, from the hem
of the mother-veil of fasting
Look into her gentle face
drink her succulent milk
Make your homeland here
Sit down right here
at the door of fasting
See how the contented hand
becomes verdant before God!
See the Eden of the soul
drenched with the daffodils of fasting!

Bashful blossom! What a wispy thing you are,
and wheeling constantly to face the sun
you're like Spring's own trapeze artiste,
so jump through the hoop of fasting!
Why so carefree and smiling, Rosebud
when you're drenched in blood?
Could you be the Isaac of God's Abraham,
delighted by the dagger of fasting?

Why so in love with bread?
see the world baked afresh
Take the wheat of spirit
Watch for the harvest of fasting

* Ghazal 2375

13

CLOSE YOUR mouth to bread – here comes the sugar of the fast*
You've seen the arts of eating, now look to the art of the fast
That king of two hundred climes will crown your head –
Hurry up and buckle on the belt of the fast

From this world like a dungeon fly up to the heights
Acquire a God's-eye view with the eyes of the fast
You majestic silver, all this while in a vat
The fire will serve you, in the sparks of the fast
Fasting is the moisture in the Zamzam well
It entered Jesus of Mary, and he reached the peak
of the fourth heaven in the journey of the fast
Think of the wings of birds and the wings of angels:
the wings of birds are strengthened eating seeds
the wings of the angels fly with fasting

If the fast is hard,
yet it has a hundred charms
It has a certain sweetness
the low blood sugar of the fast

The true fast is a mistress, veiled in her *chador*
don't look at the black cloth, but find the fast beneath it
    It makes your neck narrow
    It makes you safe from death
The results of eating: gallstones – the results of fasting: drunken buzz
Thirty days you flail
upside down and downside up
within this sea
until you reach, my master
the pearl of the fast

* Ghazal 2307

14

With all his schemes and tricks and guile
Satan's every arrow breaks
upon the shield of the fast
Fasting tells of its own charge and feint better
so close the doors of speech
and open them to the door of the fast

You are, Shams al-Haqq of Tabriz,
both patience and abstinence
you pour out sugar on days of festival
as well as the grappling of fasting

Moses, peace be upon him, and his rejection of the shepherd's prayer*

MOSES SAW a shepherd on the road
who kept crying out: O God, O Lord
 Where do I find you, that I might serve ?
 sew your moccasins, and comb your hair
 wash your clothes for you, and kill your lice
 bring milk for you, O Lord Majestic!
 Kiss your little hands and rub your feet
 and at bed time sweep your place to sleep!
 May my goats all be your sacrifice,
 in whose name I call my hoes and hies…
"Who's that you're talking with?" asked Moses,
hearing shepherd voice such silly hopes.
 "With the one who's fashioned us," he said.
 "And made earth and heavens come to light."
"What wretched state you're in!" said Moses.
"What Islam or blasphemy is that?
Total nonsense, what delusions, false!
Stuff and stop your mouth with cotton coarse!
You fill the world with stench of blaspheme
and tear faith's silken garb to tatters.
Fit for you are boots and moccasins,
but seemly for the Sun? Are such things?!
If you do not bite your lip and tongue,
flames will touch all creatures, singe the world.
If no flames fell, what's this ashen soot?
Spirit blackened and soul rejected.
If you know for sure that God is Judge,
how can you buy impudence and mud?

Masnavi Book 2: 1720–60 (following the Este'lâmi edition, lines
1724–64)

Witless friends work just like enemies –
God on high such service does not need!
You speak like this with aunt and uncle –
God's grandeur needs no ease and comfort!
Only sucklings, growing boys, drink milk
Only bare feet are for slippers fit.
And this, God's saying, means His servants:
    My servant is Me and I am him
    I fell ill, you did not visit me.
    It offended Me and not just him.
To talk like this, even of servants,
is wrong, if they "Hear and see through Me."

This talk's even nonsense in respect
of servants who "Hear and see through me."
Don't speak rudely with these men of God;
it dulls your heart, turns your pages black.
If you call some man by "Fatima"
though men and women are one specie
though this man's a calm one and serene
he'll try to slit your throat
To a woman "Fatima" is praise
to a man this cuts him like a knife
Hand and foot in our respect may fit
It's – respecting God's transcendence – spit!
He's *He neither gives birth nor was born*   [K112:3]
He creates both mother and her son
We speak of birth for forms corporal
birth flows through our world material
formed of composition and decay
contingent on a Primal Mover.
    The shepherd said, "Moses, you sewed shut
    my mouth and scorched my soul with regret."
    He rent his cloak, unleashed a hot sigh,
    bowed head into the desert, and went.

Revelation came from God to Moses:
    You've torn My servant from My presence
    Were you sent in order to unite
    or to distinguish and divide?
    Avoid if you can separation
    "More hateful still to Me, estrangement"
    I to all their qualities assign
    and give a form to their expression
    What to some is praise, to you is blame
    What's honey to his taste, your poison
    Above pure/impure I'm sanctified
    far above all suave-and boorish-ness
    I command My servants worship Me
    not for My profit, but to bless them:
    Hindus praise Me in the Hindu tongue
    Sindis praise Me in the Sindi tongue
    I'm not made pure by their remembrance
    but pure, full of pearls, do they become
    We've no regard for words or language
    We look for spirit and behavior
    We see the heart and if that's humble
    ignore the words used, brash or mumbled.

Story of a lord and his prayer-loving slave, whose communion with God in prayer and supplication was most mighty. *

A LORD, at dawn, saw need to take a bath
and shouted out, "Sonqor! wake up, let's go!
Go fetch the soap from Altun, bowl and towel;
We're heading to the baths now, no excuse!"
So Sonqor brought the nicest bowl and towel,
and off he set, together with his lord.
There was a mosque along the public way
whose call to prayer went straight in Sonqor's ears.
Sonqor was firm and fervid in his prayers,
so said, "My lord, who're always kind to slaves –
Wait here awhile beside this little shop
while I perform the rite and say the verse."

When all the people, their Imam came out,
all finished with their prayers and litanies,
Sonqor remained inside until mid-day,
his lord with eyes expectant all this while.
He called, "Sonqor! Why haven't you come out?!"
    "That Artful One won't let me come," he said;
    "Just wait, my light and lord, a little longer;
    I've not forgot – am well aware you wait!"
He waited more and called out seven times,
until exhausted by this Sonqor's trick.
    "He won't allow me leave," was his response,
    "to come outside just yet, your eminence."
"But no one's left inside the mosque!" he said.
"So who detains you, keeps you sitting there?"

* *Masnavi* Book 3: 3055–76

"The same who keeps you bound outside the door,
has likewise bound me here inside the mosque.
The one who will not let you enter in
will not give leave for me to come outside.
He who'll not let you step beyond this line
has bound this servant's foot fast on this side."

* * *

Will sea permit the fish to walk outside?
Or may earth's beasts plunge deep within the sea?
Water's source for fish, and land for beasts –
All your scheming, planning, can't undo this!
The lock is firm, unlocked by God alone –
   so reach for this: submission and content.
Were every atom turned into a key,
no opening would come except through God.
Once you forget about your planning,
you'll find your old guide brings you fortune fresh.
   Once you're forgotten to yourself, they'll mention you.
   Once you've become a slave, they'll set you free.

AN APE can mimic man in all he does*
Supposing there's no difference in the deeds
Malicious men can never comprehend:
Some men are moved by His command to act,
some (may dust pile on their heads!) by malice
Hypocrites may pray beside the pious
prompted not by abject need, but malice.
In prayer and fasting, pilgrimage and alms
both hypocrite and faithful win and lose:
To the faithful in the end goes victory
to the hypocrite, the ultimate defeat
Though both are players in a single game
They're continents apart in character.
Each proceeds his own station to assume,
moves on his designation to acquire.
Call him believer, his soul rejoices
Call him hypocrite, he's filled with fire.

* From *Masnavi* Book 1: 282–90

The Story of the Hoopoe and Solomon in explanation of "When destiny intervenes the seeing eye is closed"

WHEN SOLOMON'S royal pavilion was pitched*   [K27:15ff, 27:20]
all fowl came before him out of respect
They found he spoke their tongue and understood.
One by one with zeal each hastened to his feet.
Each bird departed from him all atwitter –
simpatico, a confidant and brother.

> A language shared brings kinship and a bond
> But talk with folk of unlike mind's a chain:
> Often Turk and Hindu can communicate
> Whereas two Turks may meet and feel estranged
> The lingo the like-minded share is best!
> Better a common heart than common tongue!
> Beyond all speech, past semaphores and scrolls,
> the heart knows many modes to transfer meanings.

Each bird told its secret arts and knowledge
boasting for Solomon of its powers …
The turn came for the hoopoe to explain
its talents, crafts and industries and thoughts
It said, "Shall I reveal a minor art
my king – keeping 'brevity is best' in mind?"
    The king said, "Tell me what that art would be."
"When I soar over all, I downward gaze
from on those heights with sharp eyes, sure of sight;
On the ground I see water in the wells –
where it is, how deep and of what color,
why it springs up, whether from soil or stone.
O Solomon, keep this always in mind
as your armies march and camp in fields afar."

Masnavi Book 1: 1202–33 (following the Este'lâmi edition, lines 1210–42)

Then Solomon replied, "My good true friend,
in wastelands where deep water's wanting
perhaps you'll locate water for the army,
and quench your fellows' thirst along the way."

The raven heard, came forward, full of envy
and said to Solomon, "His words deceive.
Talk before the king's a breach of etiquette,
especially false and foundless boasting.
Had he the constant power of sight he claims
How did he overlook the buried trap?
How did this trap, then, take him captive?
Why does he sit here, unfulfilled, encaged?"

Then Solomon demanded of the hoopoe,
"At my first taste of wine poured from your hands
is it befitting dregs should fill my mouth?
Why do you feign from milk inebriation –
in our presence, lie about your powers?"
He said, "O King, I'm but a naked beggar,
I beg, for God's sake, please don't heed my foe!
If the claims I make may seem invalid
I submit my neck to you, behead me.
The crow denies divine decree, so he's
a heretic, though his intellect's immense.
I do see traps from in the air, unless
divine decree my sight and reason cloaks.
In the face of God's decree, knowledge fades;
shadows blacken the moon, eclipse the sun.
Thus does divine decree become deployed:
It's God's decree the crow deny decree.

The tale of the grocer and his parrot and the spilling of the oil

ONCE THERE was this grocer with his parrot*
This parrot, green and sweet-of-speech, could talk
It stayed at the shop, kept watch at the door,
trading with customers witty banter.
In human converse he was eloquent,
and in parrot twitter he was expert.
One day, startled, he fluttered cross the shop,
the bottles of rose oil overturning.
From home, his master came to open shop
and sat down as an owner will, at leisure.
Finding the shop oiled and his garments soiled,
he smote the parrot's head, spilling feathers.

For several days the bird withheld from speech –
The grocer heaved a sigh from deep regret;
He plucked his beard hairs, calling out "Alas!
I've lost my lucky sun behind the fog.
Better that the hand I raised had broken
than have it smite that sweet-tongued parrot's head!"
He gave alms awhile to every dervish
in hopes his bird might rediscover speech.

After three days and nights of misery
sitting at the shop perplexed, forlorn,
showing the bird all kinds of baubles,
perchance to coax him back again to words,
there passed a mendicant, in sack-cloth dressed,
feet unshod, head shaven shiny of its hair.
The parrot opened up its mouth again
and called out like a heckler to this dervish:
"So what made you, Baldy, join the hairless?"

Masnavi Book 1: 247–65 (following the Este'lâmi edition, lines 248–66)

Been busy overturning bottled oil?"
At this assumption all burst out in laughter –
　　the bird supposed the pious monk like him!

　　Don't suppose the pure your mirror image,
　　Though it's true "ewe" and "you" may sound the same;
　　The whole world's gone astray for just this reason:
　　So few can recognize the saints of God.
　　Folks compare their own selves to the prophets,
　　and take God's saints for mortals, just like them.

PILGRIMS ON THE WAY! where are you?*
Here is the beloved, here!
Your beloved lives next door
wall to wall
why do you wander
round and round the desert?
If you look into the face of Love
    and not just at its superficial form
You yourselves become the house of God
                   and are its lords

Ten times
you trod the trek unto that house
   For once
   come into this house
   climb onto this roof
That sweet house of sanctity –
you have described its features in detail
   but now give me some indication
   of the features of its Lord
If you have seen that garden,
where is your bouquet of souvenirs?
If you are from God's sea,
where is your mother pearl of soul?

And yet, may all your troubles
   bring you treasure!
Too bad that you yourselves are veiling
   the treasures hid within

* Ghazal 648

AS I ENTER the solitude of prayer*
I put these matters to Him, for He knows
    That's my prayer-time habit, to turn and talk
    That's why it's said: "My heart delights in prayer"
Through pureness a window opens in my soul
God's message comes immediate to me
Through my window the Book, the rain and light
all pour into my room from gleaming source
    Hell's the room in which there is no window
To open windows, that's religion's goal

* From *Masnavi* Book 3: 2400–4

III

Poems on

POETRY AND MUSIC

Since your love kindled its fire in my heart
all that I owned but love for you is burnt
My studied reason and my books he shelved;
I now compose études of poetry

– Quatrain 616

The wise men tell us that we take these tunes
from the turning of celestial spheres
These sounds are revolutions of the skies
which man composes with his lyre and throat

*

We all were parts of Adam at one time
In paradise we all have heard these tunes
Though clay and water fill us up with doubts
We still remember something of those songs

*

And so, like food, samâ' *sustains God's lovers*
within its harmonies the mind's composed
imagination draws its inspiration
takes its shape within this hue and cry

– *Masnavi* Book 4: 733–43

My lover, my healer, fills the cup
Leave off then, iamb and anapest, trochee and dactyl
— from Ghazal 1367

Today, like every day, we're shot, just shot
*But do not think too hard, get the rebec (*rabâb*)!*
He whose prayer niche is the Beauty of the Friend
knows a hundred ways to pray, prostrate and bow
— Quatrain 81

BY GOD, who was from pre-eternity*
    living, knowing, powerful, self-subsisting;
whose light set ablaze the candles of love
    revealing a myriad mysteries;
who filled up the world by just one command
    with lovers and love, with ruler and ruled!
In the talismans of Shams-e Tabriz
the treasury of His wonders were concealed,
such that since the moment you departed
we've been stripped of sweetness and turned to wax –
consumed like candles, all night long we are
wedded to his flame, from his honey estranged;
In separation from his beauty, my
flesh is in ruins, my soul hoots like an owl
    Give those reins a shake in this direction
    lead joy's wild elephant here by its long trunk!
Without you present, *samâ*'s unlawful
like Satan, joy's pelted by piles of stones
Not a ghazal was composed in your absence
till your message arrived, ennobling me
The bliss of hearing your letter's music
parsed some five or six poems into verse
    May you end our darkness with your dawning,
    pride of Syria, Armence and Byzance!

* Ghazal 1760

LOOK AT me –*
these two cheeks
saffron-stained,
the worldly
multi-hued
signs of me,
and my soul,
ancient, wise,
set within
this, my frame –
     may my youth
     be as dust
     at its feet –
Look sharp now,
through my eyes –
     Do not let
my seeming
heartsomeness
steal away
with your heart.
These, my lips,
and once kissed
by their fate,
crunched out words
so sweet that
sugar blanched.
Ears will hear
the surface
of my words,
unpierced by
my soulful
thundering ...

What fires rage
in this world
from my breath,
forevers
bubble up
immortal
from my words,
evanesced?
Gazing on
Shams, the sun
     and the pride
     of Tabriz,
what was it
I saw that
set all these –
     my meanings –
in motion?

* Ghazal 2077

MY SUN and moon has come, my ears and eyes have come*
That smooth and argent skin, that mine of gold has come!
A dizzy warmth whelmed my head, light lit up my eyes –
What else that you could ever ask, that too has come!
That bandit, breaker of repenting vows has come!
That jasmine-bodied Joseph, sudden at my side!
Today beats yesterday, my friend of auld lang syne,
and I was drunk last night, since news of him had come.
The one I sought for yesterday, a lamp in hand –
Today, like wildflowers, just swept into my hands!
He cinched me hard in his embrace with both his arms;
what a precious belt that gorgeous monarch gave me!
See his garden: fresh spring! His vintner: drunken eyes!
See his tasty, sweet-melt rose-petal marmalade
I'm not fearing death, since that fount of life has come –
Why fear barbs and jabs, since he has become my shield?
    I'm Solomon today, since you gave me this ring
    and a royal crown has come to rest upon my head
When pain became unbearable in love, I left.
O Lord, what blessed bliss has come to me by travel!

    Time's come to drink the wine and lighting-bolt my mind
    Time's come to soar aloft, since wings have come to me
    Time's come for me to shine like sun upon this world
    Time's come for me to roar aloud, a virile lion!
    Two lines remain unsung, but love, I'm borne away
    to where the world appears to me as summary

* Ghazal 633

"Song of the Reed"

LISTEN TO this reed*
play out its plaint
unfold its tale
of separations:

Ever since they cut me
from my reedy bed,
   my cry
makes men and women
   weep
I like to keep my breast
fretted with loss
to convey
the pain of longing
   All those severed from their roots
   thirst to return to the source
I raise my plaint in any kind of crowd,
in front of both the blessed and the bad.
They hear in me just what they want to hear –
None tries to find my secrets couched within
My secret's soon divulged in my lament
but eyes and ears lack light, cannot discern it
   Not flesh from soul, nor soul from flesh are veiled,
   but none is granted leave to see the soul.

Fire, not breath, makes music through that reed –
Let all who lack that fire be blown away!
What races through the reed is love's own fire
What bubbles in the wine is love's ferment
The reed, soother to all sundered lovers –
its piercing modes reveal our hidden pain:

Masnavi Book 1: 1–34

   (What's like the reed, poison and antidote,
     soothing as it pines and yearns away?)
The reed tells the tale of a blood-stained quest
singing legends of love's mad obsessions
    Only the swooning know such awareness
    only the ear can comprehend the tongue

             * * *

In our sadness time slides by listlessly
the days searing inside us as they pass.
But so what if the days may slip away?
So long as you, Uniquely Pure, abide.
    Within this sea drown all who drink but fish
    If lived by bread alone, the day seems long
    No raw soul ever kens the cooked one's state
    So let the talk of it be brief; go, peace!

    Break off your chains
    My son, be free!
    How long enslaved
    by silver, gold?
    Pour the ocean
    in a pitcher,
    can it hold more
    than one day's store?
    The pitchers of
    the greedy-eyed
    never seem full.
    Only once closed
    in contentment
    does the oyster
    produce a pearl.

He whom love runs ragged and haggard
gets purged of all his faults and greed

Welcome, Love! Sweet salutary suffering,
physician-healer of our maladies!
Cure of our pride
of our conceits,
Our Plato
Our Galen!
By Love
our earthly flesh
ascends to heaven
Our mountains
are made supple,
moved to dance.
   Love moved Mount Sinai, my love,
   and *it made Moses swoon*.   [K7:143]

* * *

Let me just touch those harmonious lips
and I, reed-like, will tell what may be told
   A man may know a myriad of songs
   but cut from those who know his tongue, he's dumb.
   Once the rose wilts and the garden fades
   the nightingale will no more sing his tune.

The Beloved is all; the lover, veil.
The Beloved's alive; the lover, carcass.
Unsuccored by Love, the poor lover is
a bird all plucked, grounded and unfeathered.
Without the Beloved's surrounding light
how perceive what's ahead and what's gone by?

Love desires these words to be revealed;
if no mirror reflects them, who's at fault?
Do you know why your mirror won't reflect?
Because unburnished, dross obscures the face.

DO YOU get what the rebec is saying*
about flowing tears
about insides seared by love?
   I'm a skin, peeled off its muscle
   Torn off and tormented, why shouldn't I wail?
Its neck also says:
   A verdant branch, I was
   tall in my saddle until
   uprooted, splintered by that knight

We are exiles torn from our roots!
Hear this from me, ye kings:
To God is the return   [K3:12]
We first sprouted in this world from Truth
and to it we return as the cycle revolves
Our cry (just like a thunderbolt in gathered rainclouds
         just like a caravan's departure bell):
Seeker!
   Do not get heartset on any station on the way
   or you'll be hurt when it comes time to pull away
   for you have come traversing many stages
   from conception to the fullness of youth
Take it easy, so you may escape with ease,
   give freely and receive a just reward
Hold firmly to Him, as He holds firmly to you
   In the beginning: Him
   In the end: Him
   Find: Him

* Ghazal 304

His bow sets Lovers' hearts
   aquiver
   and so he draws
   the spiked fiddle's strings
   in slow vibrato
Whether the lover be Arab, Greek or Turk
this call speaks to him, rings true
The winds lament, calling to you:
   Come, follow me to the stream
   I was water, I turned to wind, I came
   to free the thirsty from this mirage

That is the logos of wind that once was water
and will return to water when the veils fall off
This cry was heard beyond all dimensions of time and space:
   Flee dimensionality, but never turn your face from me!
   Lover, you're not less than a moth
   And a moth never flees the flame

The king's within the citadel
because of my owlish spectre
How can I leave the city for a roost in ruins?
   When an ass goes mad
   crack its head with an ox whip until its smarts return
If I humor him, it will only make more thistles for him
   Of the infidels, He has said they deserve:
   smiting upon the neck   [K47:4]

THE SEA OF HONEY sent word to me this morning:*
   See this wave on wave of honey?
      To people's eyes they are ghazals
While fasting, one drinks in only the sound of water
And yet, eventually, that sound does its work
Samâ' is the gurgle of water as the thirsty dance
You'll come to life with this call of babbling water
Water says: you've grown from me, you'll come to me
   You'll return at last to where you first were
I swear by your precious head!
If any of this water spills on the head
even one that's bald
a musk-black tangle of tufts will sprout

The imbiber did not mix the wine with this water
He'll be hungover on and on. Just wait, you'll see.

* Ghazal 1357

THEY DANCE, parade about the battlefield*
    they dance in their own blood, all true men do.
When they free themselves from their own clutches
when they can leap right out of their own flaws:
    they clap their hands and then they do a dance
Within their breasts a beat like minstrels' drums
    and all the oceans foam with their ferment
You cannot see it with your outward eyes
    but even leaves on trees sprout hands for them
the leaves keep clapping to their beat – but listen
    for this with your inner (not your body's) ear.

* From *Masnavi* Book 3: 96–100

IV

Poems of

SILENCE

I met last night in stealth with Wisdom's elder
begged him to divulge in full life's secrets
This he softly, softly whispered in my ear:
It must be seen, it can't be told, so hush!

– Quatrain 1035

The way of the middle is wisdom's path
But what is that middle? It's relative ...
Ten prostrations of prayer may wear you out,
while five hundred may work just fine for me.
One man walks barefoot clear to the Kaaba,
one knocks himself out to the corner mosque.
One man gives his life without second thoughts,
and one it kills to give a loaf of bread!
A mean is derived only from finites,
since we can measure beginning to end –
the beginning and end are requisites
for mind to encompass average and mean.
But In the Beginning and In the End
remain unexplained by anyone.
"Were the sea ink for my Lord," *says the Book ...*

Yes, even were all Seven Seas turned ink
still hopeless, infinitely incomplete!
Cut down all gardens, groves, for pens; still we'd
not come one word closer to definition –
that mass of pen and ink would pass away
the tale, unfathomed, would go on and on
                                   – Masnavi Book 2: 3531–6

I SERVE THAT ORB in heaven, say no word but Orb*
Speak to me of nothing but sweetness and light
Not of bother, but of treasure
And if you cannot find the words,
don't bother.

Yesterday a craze came over me
   Love saw, came up to me:
   Here I am,
   don't shout,
   don't rip your shirt,
   hush, shh!
I spoke: Love, I'm scared of that other thing.
   There is no other thing, say nothing!
   I will whisper secrets in your ear
   you just nod in asseveration
   speak in semaphore

A nova, a celestial love,
burst bright above the heartway
So exquisite the quest of heart,
it cannot be expressed
I asked: Heart, what orb is this?
   Heart intimated:
   Beyond fathom –
   be quiet, forget!
Is this the face of man or angel?
   Beyond men and angels
   hush!
What is it!? Tell me, I'm in a whirl
   Whirl on, keep quiet!
   You sit within this room

* Ghazal 2219

whose walls reflect
mere forms and suppositions
Get up, go out, move on,
keep quiet!
I said: Heart, befather me!
Does this not match with God's description?
Yes, my son, it does,
but do not tell.

MUSICIAN, FACE moonrise bright –*
Tell us, what was it that you heard?
    Here you are among friends; you can
Tell us everything you saw.
    Our king and crown
    our realm of joy!
    Within the sanctum
    of the one who animates us
Tell us, what did you come across?
    The languid drunken eyes
    of one whose company God keeps?
    Last night in his bed of roses,
Tell us, what was it that you picked?

    You slipped through my clutches
    I lost hold of my tipsy heart
    You who have seen it all,
    which one did you choose?
Tell us!
    The seasons come and go
    but your festival
    goes on and on forever
    How in the world
    did you escape unaided
    from heaven's inexorable turning wheel?
Tell us!

    I sank, sugar,
    into the soul's fields of cane
Tell us if you tasted of its sweets
    Wine pulls me left
    heart pulls me right
    What a pleasant pushing-pulling!
Tell us what repelled or pulled you?

* Ghazal 2245

45

You brim the goblet up with wine
disturb the peace, inciting riot
Tell us, how did you get the key to tavern doors?
Ferment of our tavern
radiance of our prayers
you who strip naked our desires,
Tell us!

The moon in the sky
darkens, debased by clouds
You, orb untouched, beyond the clouds
Tell us!
May your shade forever shelter us,
may your moon always beam bright,
may the wheel of heaven heed your wishes;
Tell us what has made you bolt and shy away?

Love asked
how did you fall for me in love last night?
I said
Don't beat around the question how,
what tapestry is this you've woven?
Tell us.
I was cautious
ascetic, a man at war with sin
Why did you fly away to safety
like a bird?
Tell us ...

THIS HOUSE where the lute strings constantly strum –*
  ask of its lord, what house is this?
If this is the house of the Kaaba
how can it be so full of icons?
If this house is a Magian fane
how can the light of God be shining here?
There's a treasure in this house
too great for galaxies to hold
  "House" and "lord"
  are just a play, divertimento
  Don't touch the House –
    this house is talisman
  Don't speak to the lord –
    he's drunk all night

  Musk and fragrance, the dust and thistles of this house
  Verse and melody, the cries arising from this house
  To sum up
  he who gains entry to this house is
  Sultan of the earth
  Solomon of the age
My lord, kindly look down here
from your perch upon the parapet
for those soft cheeks
are touched by
constant fortune's kiss
By your life!
all else but the vision of your face –
  even ownership of earth –
to me is so much hocus pocus

  The rose bower, baffled
  wonders: what petals, what blossoms, these?

* Ghazal 332

The birds, bewitched
twitter: what bait, what trap is this?

This is the lord of the sphere:
   an orb like the Moon or Venus
and this is the house of love:
   boundless, uncontained

Like a mirror to the soul
your visage fills the heart
the heart, like the comb
tangles in your tress
In the presence of Joseph –
   there where the ladies cut their hands
meet me, love
for my soul's somewhere in that space
All the house is drunk:
none knows what gives
nor minds who comes, who goes

   Well, don't sit there on the doorstep –
   it's an omen that invites an ill
   come, quickly, in the house
   He who stands at thresholds
   darkens doorsteps

   God's drunkards, though a multitude
   are no more than one
   while the passion-drunk
   are dualist, trinitarian

   Charge into the lion's thicket
   unafraid of mauling
   for fearful thoughts
   are a sissy's plague

Love and mercy –
and not mauling
await you there
But standing outside the door
your suppositions
bar you like a bolt
Don't set fire to this thicket
be silent, heart!
hold your tongue
for your tongue
is a lick of flame.

I CALL UPON you*
   who practice ceaseless sorcery
   who make a lion a gazelle
   whose magic conjures double vision
   who makes our hands to rub our eyes
   who makes the sour citron
      change its colors
      to ripen into sweeter plums
Your magic makes the lamb a wolf
   makes a wheatspike barley corn
Your magic makes imagination's scroll unfold
   into proclamations of immortality
Touched by your sorcery
   even the wayward pagan's beard
   billows in the breeze of wisdom

Your sorcery's made a sophist of me
   You who with your marshaled truculence
   Moslemize humanity, Turkify all Hinduality
In the heat of battle you transform
the mammoth tusky elephant into a gnat
Then let them join in even combat –
   destiny against divine decree
   till one emerges true

Enough of sophistry:
Hold my peace!
Unleash the tongue of meaning

* Ghazal 116

WHEN THE SUN came out*
from the pit
of a black well,
hear this call
in each and every beam:
    There is no God but God!
        No, not beams ...
he came out as sun-soul
stealing the bright garb
and halo from the sun
When the heart's orb
came out Adam-like
from clay and water –
    A hundred suns like Joseph
    sink into the well

Lift a head from the dust,
you're not less than an ant
Give tidings to the ants
of fields and crops
Ignorant of our luscious hyacinth
the ant contents itself with rotted grain
Tell the ant:
it's spring, you have hands and feet –
Won't you wend your way from graves to meadows?

Why speak of tiny ants?
Even Solomon himself
rent his garb in longing!
    (O God! do not lay hold of me
    for these metaphors that mar and jar!

* Ghazal 2408

But the tailor cuts the cloth
to fit the customer
my garment's long
but then the customer is short.
Bring me one of standing
and we'll cut a cloth so long
that the thread that holds the moon will snap)

I'll keep silence from now on
for in my silence
Truth and error separate
just like wheat from chaff

THE HEART like grain*
us like a mill
   how can the mill
   know why it turns?
Flesh, like the stone
water, our thoughts
Stone says: It knows
   the course, Water.
and Water says:
   Ask the miller;
   he sends water
   cascading down.
Miller tells you:
   Chewer of bread
   if not for this
   how bake, how eat?
And on and on
the cycle goes

Silence! Ask God
for He'll tell you.

* Ghazal 181

V

Poems of

LOSS AND CONFUSION

Tell for a while
the tale of Tabriz
Tell for a while
the bloodthirsty tale
of an eye-fluttering flirt
How bitter to be
severed from such sugary lips –
spoon out the candy
of those godly sugars

– from Ghazal 807

We've left our job and craft and store in flames
We've learned ghazals and lyrics, lines of verse
In love, he's heart and soul, our very eyes
We've left all three – heart, soul and eyes – in flames

– Quatrain 1293

GO LAY YOUR HEAD on your pillow, let me be alone*
   leave me laid waste to wander the night, afflicted
Me and the waves of grief, alone, dusk to dawn
   Come be kind, if you will; go and be cruel, if you want.
Leave me, run, fast, or you'll fall likewise in affliction
   Choose the more wholesome path and leave harm's way
Me and the puddle of my eyes, huddled in sorrow's corner
   turning mill after mill after mill with my tears

Impudent, brazen, he murders me, stony his heart
none dares demand money to atone my blood
The monarch of handsome faces is under no duty to be true
   Sallow-faced lover, be patient, be true
   It is a pain cured only by dying
   I cannot tell you how to treat this pain

Last night I dreamt I saw an old man in the street of love
   he beckoned me with his hand, "Come this way, to me"
If a dragon blocks the path, love works like an emerald
   The glittering of the emerald will repulse the dragon

      Enough! I am senseless,
      If your skills can match the task
      Tell the dates of Bu Ali
      and box the ears of Bu Alâ

* Ghazal 2039

IT'S STRANGE! Where'd that gorgeous heartbreaker go?*
Odd – where'd our tall and supple cypress go?
He bathed us like a candle in his light,
in thin air vanished, left us! Where'd he go?
My heart, leaf-like, trembles all day long at this:
At midnight, all alone, where'd that heart-throb go?

Run up to the road and ask the travelers –
    That soul-quickening companion, where'd he go?
Walk to the garden, ask the gardeners –
    That luscious bough of rosebuds, where'd he go?
Clamber on the roof and ask the watchmen –
    Our one and only monarch, where'd he go?

A man possessed, I wander in the plain
crying, "Where in the world d'our gazelle go?
My tearful eyes outflow the mighty Oxus –
    That pearl sank in this sea, where did it go?
All night through I beg the Moon and Venus –
    Where did, in heaven's name, that bright orb go?

Since he's ours, how is it he's with others?
Since he's not here, from here to where'd he go?
And if he's left the world of clay and breath,
his placeless soul to join with God did go.
So tell me clear:
    Shams al-Din of Tabriz
    who quotes "The Sun dieth not" –
    Where'd he go?

* Ghazal 677

I'M MAD about, just crazy*
   for Damascus!
My heart feels melancholic and
   I left my spirit in Damascus!
Blissful morn comes up in that direction
Dawn and dusk, intoxicated
   by Damascene bewitchments:
Love bereft, we stand by Barid Gate
Beyond the Lovers' Mosque
   in the green field of Damascus
Have you never sipped the Spring of Bu Nuwas?
We love the quenching water
   of Damascus!
Let me swear an oath on Uthman's Codex:
   That heart-stealing pearl makes
   us sparkle in Damascus
Far from the Gate of Release
   and the Gate of Paradises
   you can't imagine what visions we see
   in Damascus
Let's climb Ribwa, and on Christ's Cradle
we'll be like monks, drunk on the dark red wines
   of Damascus
In regal Nayrab we saw a tree;
   sitting in its shade, we're dizzied
     by Damascus
We roll through her Verdant Field, struck
   like polo balls by mallet curls of hair,
     on the quadrangle of Damascus
   We could never lack for Mizza, for we gain savor and delight
   at the Eastern Gate of Damascus
On Righteous Mountain is a mine of gems
   through which we swim in the jewels of Damascus

* Ghazal 1493

58

Since Damascus is paradise of the world,
    we long for a vision of the fair angels of Damascus
For a third time let's speed to Syria from Byzance
For tresses dark as Syrian nights
    drench us in the fragrance of Damascus

If that is where to practice servitude
    to Shams al-Haqq of Tabriz
      then my heart's mastered by Damascus,
      and mister, I'm Master of Damascus!

NIGHT AND day*
buffeted by fantasies of you
head planted at your pedestal
night and day
Day and night
I'll keep this up
until I drive
the night and day
to love distraction

They demanded from the lovers
earnest heart and soul
I make pledges day and night
with heart and soul
Until I discover
what is in my brain
I'll not scratch my head for a time
day and night

Your love plays me
like a tune
day and night
Sometimes harpstring, sometimes lyre
you work me over
with your plectrum
day and night
My high quivering notes
scale the skies
you poured out forty-fold libations
for all mankind
from that ferment
I'm sotted night and day

* Ghazal 302

You drive a train of choke-reined lovers
I walk in those chains
smashed, pulling your weight
I stagger like a burdened camel
day and night

Unless I break fast with your sugar
I'll keep hungry day and night
until the judgment
My fortune will celebrate a festival
when I break fast at bounty's table
day and night
but the festival befalls us
only once in every year
I'm feted
with your full face
each new moon
night and day

Life of the night
pulse of the day –
you animator
me anticipation –
night and day
All anticipation
counting hours
day and night
until the tryst day
and the night you promised

He sowed such warmth
in my thirsty soul
I rain down tears
from my cloudy eyes
night and day

I MANAGE FINE with no others around;*
I cannot manage without you
  My heart bears your brand,
  it won't wander away from you
  Reason's eye blurs with your wine
  heaven's wheel spins under your thumb
  Pleasure's nose follows your lead
I cannot manage without you
  Psyche ferments at your mention
  The heart drinks nectar from your hand
  and reason lets out with the roar:
I cannot manage without you
  My potion and intoxication,
  my flowering time, my garden bloom,
  my sleep, my peace
I cannot manage without you
  My pomp, my presence, dominion, wealth!
  You are my crystal water and
I cannot manage without you
  You alternate between
  being true and being cruel
  You're mine – where are you off to?
I cannot manage without you
  They offer heart, you snatch it
  they vow, repent, you break it
  All this and more you do
I cannot manage without you
  If only the world were inverted
  We could live without you –
      there where Eden's garden is Gehenna

* Ghazal 553

I cannot manage without you
    If you're head, I stand pat, your foot
    If you're palm, I'm in hand, your flag
    If you go, I'm undone, a no-thing
I cannot manage without you
    You've charmed me from my sleep
    you've washed me clear away
    You've cut me off from all
I cannot manage without you
    If you will not be my partner
    my affairs are all ashambles!
    My counselor, my consoler –
I cannot manage without you
    Living lacks joy without you
    dying lacks joy without you
    How can I clear my mind of care for you?
I cannot manage without you
    Whatever I say, my source,
    reveals my strengths and faults
    So please, be gracious!
    and repeat with me:
I cannot manage without you.

VI

Poems from

DISCIPLE TO MASTER

I once was an ascete – you made me sing
made me riot of the party – drunk with wine
You found me on a prayer rug, dignified –
made me toy for children, taunted on my block

– Quatrain 1716

I HAVE THIS friend*
I have this cave   [K9:40]
I am gutted by love
you are that friend
you are that cave
   my lord, don't cast me off
you are Noah you are numen
you are conqueror you are conquest
you are the breast laid open   [K94:1]
   I stand at the door of mysteries
you are light
you are festival
you are fortune, God-confirmed
you're the bird of Mount Sinai
   I the wounded captive in your beak

a drop you are
the sea you are
grace you are
wrath you are
sugar, poison you are you are
   do not afflict me any longer!
You are the solar sign
the house of Venus
the paradise of hope
   let me in, my Friend
You are daylight
you are fasting
you are the wages of our begging
You are water you are jug
   let this lover drink!

* Ghazal 37

66

You are bait
you are the trap
You are wine
you are the cup
you are cooked
you are raw
 Please do not leave me raw!

If this flesh would stop its spinning
 my heart would not be robbed so dizzy
you left town
 so I would not prattle on incessantly

O JOSEPH (sweet the name!)*
  is that you walking sweetly overhead
    along the roof?

Shatterer of my chalice
  Destroyer of my traps
    my light, my festival
      my victorious fortune!
        Stir up my ferment
          that my grapes may wine.

Thief of my heart and
  my highest aspiration
    where I turn to worship
      object of my adoration
        You've lit up my incense
          watch the smoke rise from me
            My friend, my defrauder
              seducer of my drunken heart!
                Don't kick the legs out from under me
                Take my turban as my earnest

My heart got stuck in mud
up to its ankles
But I'd trade my life,
not just my heart.
    What fires burn the lovesick heart?
    So much for it,
    so much for me!

* Ghazal 4

ICON, I CAN NEVER get my fill of you*
and yet breath by breath I'm fed up with separation
I see how content you are with our discomfiture
How can I, heartlorn lover, get my discomfited fill?
My dropsied heart drinks gulps of blood
my eyes are ever wet and filled with tears

    If you're fed up with this world, come –
    none ever gets his fill from that world of mine

When I saw all your lovers in agreeable accord
I felt full of nullus, negative and no;
yet with your breath, love's Israfil, a resurrecting trumpet blows –
I cannot get my fill of spirit-blast, its clarion rise and fall.
When the scent of Soul's goblet met my brain
O soul of Soul, I found Jamshid's grail so unfulfilling
Since this madness waxes hour by hour
only the miser remains unfilled by more-and-less
When I saw his cup and glass, I felt
I'd had my full of the inverted multi-layered globe
The image of Shams of Tabriz appears –
    I cry uncle for his beauty
    I swear I've had my fill of kith and kin.

* Ghazal 1046

I PAINT ICONS*
All the time
I am forging an idol
and then
in front of your eyes
I melt down all the idols
I conjure myriad forms
infuse them with spirit
When I see your form
I cast them all in flames
Are you
    wine-pouring vintner?
    foe to consciousness?
    or sworn to destroy each home that I build?
Spirit is poured over you, mingled with you
Since your scent oozes spirit
well then, let me caress it
All blood that flows from me
calls out to your dust:
    I share the same tint as your affection
    I'm playmate to your love

In this home of water and clay
my heart is in shambles without you
Enter this home, beloved
or I will abandon the house.

* Ghazal 1462

I SLEEP AND WAKE in love's afflictions*
my heart turns on the spit of passion's fire
If you abandoned me to best refine me,
You're wisdom, without you I'm unrefined
Why the harshness in your cruel heart? How long
must I cry and suffer what has happened?
Because I love to say "I'll die for you"
I live in you and call myself "your kill"
You counseled patience as my consolation?
   (Don't suppose they always loved with patience!)
The moment you left, absence would kill me
if each day I did not expect to meet you.
I repent prayerfully, beseechingly
to my lord for my sins and shortcomings
   Tabriz radiates with my lord, Faith's Sun;
   I weep blood, choke on it, for what I've done.

* Ghazal 319

71

MY LIFEBLOOD, my world,*
where were you last night?
   No, what am I saying –
   You were within our hearts.
Last night there was cruelty in your separation
You had been a paragon of faithfulness
   What a state I was in last night!
   Whose company were you in last night?
I'm envious. I wish I were a tunic –
the arms of a tunic held you in tight embrace.
   I haven't got the gall to ask you
   "Why were you absent from gloomy me?"
Swift-souled lover, when you slipped away
you flew off like the breeze at dawn
Trouble and toil bound my hands without you
Stay, because you have been a slave to trouble.
Your cheeks' high color gives you away, you know
   You were in the sanctuary of God's grace
You have your own color,
unsullied by earthly colors
You're one color with immortality
You are mirror
your color is Someone's reflection
You were untinted by all color

* Ghazal 3165

LOVER, COME here. Today you are ours*
Where are you where are you where are you?
I swear by your victorious insignia,
and the royal shade of your divine wings
    We are like the sun! You are
Bird of Royal Omen, Royal Bird, Royal Bird!
The mortal world is no more; within it you're
immortal, immortal, immortal
The world strums you as harmonious harp
you tune it, in tune, in tune
When the lover loses his shirt, for him
you're tunic you're tunic you're tunic
I fall silent, but for God's sake
be like God be like God, like God

* Ghazal 2716

VII

Poems from

MASTER TO DISCIPLE

Come here, I have no designs on you, you understand?
It's no good to stay over there, why be all alone?
All life comes from the Chelebi of the path;
   find God, what are you following?
The Chelebi wants his charges;
   what do you make of the Chelebi?

— from Ghazal 1982

Essence: Poverty — all else: attribute
Good health: Poverty — all else: disease
All the world's delusion and deception
From this world Poverty's our goal and treasure

— Quatrain 1042

DO YOU, novice, wish to turn dung to musk?*
Then graze the garden many years. You must!
Don't chomp on hay and barley like an ass;
    Like musk deer, graze the redbud in Khotan
    Graze jasmine or on clove, or rose alone
    Go to the fields of Khotan with that flock
    Get your gut accustomed: Sweet basil, rose.
    You'll taste sagacity, prophetic might
    So wean your stomach-juice off barley, straw
    Your regimen is rose, sweet basil – Start!
The body's stomach calls us to the trough,
    the belly of the heart to basil sweet.
Hay and barley-eaters go for slaughter
    imbibe the light of Truth, become Koran
    Half of you is musk
and half dung, watch out!
    Amass that Chinese musk
don't fill with dung!

* From *Masnavi* Book 5: 2472–9

TAKE LOVE'S chalice and on you go*
just choose this as your love and go
Be limpid wine, pure as spirit
unblurred by vinestalk scum, and flow
 One glance at him's worth scores of lives
 strike a bargain, sell your soul and go
 Such a body: argent, fluid, fine!
 pay the silver, close your purse, and go
Let the whole world weep for you! So what?
Look up at his smiling globe and go.
If they call you hypocrite, poseur,
Say "So I am, and ten times worse," and go
Thumb your nose at people, rub it in
suck the sugar of his lips and go –
 "The moon is mine, the rest is yours
 I need neither hearth nor home," you go
  Who is that moon?
  Lord of Tabriz, it's Shams, the Sun!
  Step into his regal shade
  Let's go!

* Ghazal 2179

DIDN'T I TELL you:*
    Don't go over there, for I am the one who knows you;
    In this mirage of annihilation,
    I am your source of life;
    and if in anger for a million years
    you run from me, in the end you will return to me
    for I am your destination?
Didn't I tell you:
    Don't be content with the outer scheme
    and semblance of the world,
    for I am the architect
    of your pavilion of contentment?
Didn't I tell you:
    I am the sea and you are just a fish in me;
    don't go on the dry and sandy beach
    for I am your liquid purity?
Didn't I tell you:
    Don't step into a trap just like a bird.
    Come to me, for I am your wings and feathers
    and your power of flight?
Didn't I tell you:
    They will rob you and leave you cold,
    for I am your hearth and fire?
Didn't I tell you:
    They will fill you with ugly attributes
    so that you will lose your way to me,
    your wellspring of virtues, attributes?
Didn't I tell you:
    Don't say how or from which quarter
    your affairs will be arranged;
    I create you out of nowhere and of nothing?

* Ghazal 1725

If you are the lamp of hearts,
know which way leads homeward.
And if you have the qualities of a lord,
know that
I
am
your
Overlord.

AND WHO   He asked   is at the door?*
I said   The humblest of your servants
              State your business! he demanded
My lord   I said   to greet you.
How long   He asked   will you keep knocking?
I said   Until you answer
He asked   How long will you ferment?
I said   Until the Resurrection

              I boasted of bravery and dominion
              and how I let them go for love
He warned   The Judge will call for you to prove your claims
I said   My tears come freely forth, eye-witnesses
                  I submit the pallor of my face as evidence
He said   Your evidence is inadmissible
                   your witnesses both blurred and tainted
I said   By your majestic justice! They testify
                   both fair and true
He said   Who came here with you?
I replied   O King, just the image I carry of you.
He asked   Who summoned you here?
I answered   The fragrance in your chalice
He demanded   State your purpose
Friendship   I responded   and fidelity
He asked   What is it that you want from me?
I said   Your universal grace
He countered   There is a place more pleasant. Name it!
I replied   The Royal Palace
And what   He queried   did you see there?
I said   A million blessings
And why   He asked   is it now desolate?
I said   For fear of robbers.
And who   He asked   is a robber?

* Ghazal 436

I said   The robber is reproach
He said   And where can one take refuge?
In continence   I replied   and piety
He asked   And what is continence
I said   The way to safety and salvation
He asked   And which way lies calamity?
                        In the pathway of my love to you
                        And how will you manage there?
                        By being steadfast ...
Silence!   For if I tell you of his attributes
                        you will lose yourself
                        and find yourself
                        homeless
                    completely without prospects

HERE A FEW, there a few*
the drunkards all show up
the worshipers of wine
one by one turn up
along the way, heartmelters
all along they flow and flirt
smooth and pink-cheeked boys
arriving from the rose bowers
Little by little
in the world's egress-regress
beings come and nothings go
pockets all loaded up
like mines with gold
they come to visit those of empty-hand

You gaunt and battle-wearied of love's pastures!
Here come the hale and fattened up reserves
The pure of soul, like beams of sun,
shine down from up above on earthly ones
Blessed the garden as it bears
fresh fruits in winter
for all the Marys
   Kindness their origin
   and to kindness they return
   coming from rose bower
   to a bower of rose

* Ghazal 819

CARAVANEER! See the camels all on down the line, a whole train, drunk:*
    the lead drunk, the lord drunk, the friend drunk, the rest drunk
Gardner! Thunder makes our music, the clouds pour out our wine.
They make:
    gardens drunk and hill-slopes drunk, the buds drunk, the thorns drunk
Spinning heavens! Stop a while and see the turning of the elements:
    water, drunk – the wind, drunk – the earth, drunk – and fire, drunk.

What brings about a scene like this, and what true meaning lies beneath?
Don't ask!
    the spirit's drunk – reason, drunk – fancy, drunk – mystery, drunk!
Now cut it out, all this compulsion! Be humbler than the dust and you'll
    behold through the compelling God: each speck of dust, drunk
So don't be thinking, "the gardens lack drunkenness in winter's dead" –
    for a spell they'll hide from scheming eyes, drunk.
The roots of all those trees are sipping up a covert wine;
    just wait a day or two, and they'll awaken, drunk!

When jostled by these passing drunkards, do not get upset:
    with thundering music and drenching wine, how could they keep in line?
Saqi! Pour us a singular, united wine – why all this bickering?
    friends drunk on affirmation and foes on denial, drunk
Stir up the wind's incantations over us to untwine this knot:
    until wine fills these heads, they'll never pawn their turbans, drunk
Is our Saqi stingy, then, or are these evaporating wines?!
    Neither holds steady as the mounts list onward, drunk.
Look on these sallowed faces and pour out rosy wine
    for there is no rose in the cheeks and faces of the drunk
You have a divine wine most subtle and smooth to swallow
    If he wants, each day a cellar-full he'll drink, the drunk
Shams of Tabriz, not a single soul around you's sober –
    the infidel, the believer: smashed; the ascete, the vintner: drunk!

* Ghazal 390

WHOEVER LEAVES our circle for another place*
    might as well relinquish sense of sight and sound
A lover licks his liver's blood, lion-like;
    what lion-heart would shrink from love and guts?
Hearts suck up cruelty from heart-throbs like cubes of sugar;
    did you ever see a parrot turn from sugar?
It's a small gnat that turns at every headwind
    Only stealthy thieves scatter in moonlight.

Any head that the Lord strikes dumb or scrambles
    drops its place in heaven and heads for hellfire.
And he who fathoms death leaps to welcome death
    rushes for the robe, crown and realm eternal.
Fate decrees that so-and-so will die abroad
    and fear of the reaper spurs him from his home
Enough of stalking such unbecoming prey!
    for the night and its phantoms flee from the dawn.

* Ghazal 794

YOU WHO SUPPOSED steam*
to be spirit
mistook gold druck
for mine lode
You who
sink in the earth like Korah
believing earth is sky
You who looked on puppet plays of demons
and mistook them for humans
From you love recoils
for loathsomeness
though you suppose
yourself involved
You
eyes teared
with pagan soot
imagining soot
shining light
You
like a worm
squirming
in lust's filth
supposing
lovers act the same.
Lust drunkenness, the curse's mark –
You who
confuse the Traceless
with a common mark
You
rotted amid words and sounds
You who suppose God tongueless, dumb

* Ghazal 2382

The moon beams down
on your blind lunacy
You who
imagine the moon eclipsed

   All I have said
   I address to myself,
You who
have assumed
this an attack on others ...

VIII

Poems of

MASTER TO MASTER

I am declawed by love of Shams-e Din
or else would I restore sight to the blind
So you, Truth's Light, Hosam al-Din, cure him
and may it blind the evil envious eye!
                                        — Masnavi Book 2: 1122–3

Pillar and haven of the morn, it's dawn
Pardon me to my master, Hosam al-Din!
                                        — Masnavi Book 1: 1807

A hundred thousand hidden monarchs
raise up their heads so proud in realms beyond
Their names concealed – He is a jealous God!
Not every beggar should pronounce their names!
                                        — Masnavi Book 2: 931–2

I WAS DEAD, came back to life*
I wept, began to laugh
Love's force came over me
Fortune smiled on me forever
My eye has seen its fill
my spirit feels no fear
I have a lion's gall
I'm luminous as Venus!
   You are not mad, he said
   You are not fit for this home
I went mad, was bound by chains

   You are not drunk, he said
   You don't belong among us, go
I went and got drunk, stuffed with joy

   You are not slain, he said
   You are not buried in joy
Before his vivifying face I fell down, dead

   You are too clever by half, he said
   drunk with doubt and fantasy
I got deceived, stunned, cut off from all

   You glow like a candle, he said
   the focus of our common adoration
I'm not together
I'm no candle
I'm dispersed like wisps of smoke

   You're a shaykh and guide, he said
   Go ahead and lead the way

* Ghazal 1393

I'm no shaykh
am not ahead
I am slave to your command

You have wings and feathers, he said
I need not give you means of flight
In yearning for his wings and feathers
I am clipped and plucked

New-found fortune told me:
Do not go away, do not take offense
for I am coming towards you
out of grace and kindness
Old love said to me:
Do not leave my side
Alright, I won't, I said
I've become grounded, abiding

You are the source of the rays of the sun
I am the shade beneath the willow tree
Since your rays hit my head, I've drooped, melted.
The radiant spirit touched and cleft my heart,
opened it, my heart. It spun a fresh silk,
my heart, made me enemy to these rags
In bliss the soul's form boasted on at dawn:
I was slave and bondsmen
I've become king and lord!
Paper I touch to write you cries sweet thanks
for it feels your endless sugar in me.
Base earth gives thanks for heaven's bowl inverted
that light rains through its turning apertures
Heaven's wheel thanks angels, king, dominion –
through His gifts and grace I'm brightness, bounty!
God's gnostic gives his thanks for eminence:
"a star above the seven spheres, I shine"

I was Venus, I am the moon
   I become celestial wheel
   with countless levels
I was Joseph, and now I engender Josephs

You've made me, brightest moon!
   Gaze into me and in yourself
for the traces of your smile
   have turned me to a field of laughing blossoms

Like a chess game
Be in motion
silent but expressive
For in castling with the world King
   how regal and auspicious
   I have become!

YOU THERE, checkmated by the king of love*
Don't be moved to wrath or retribution
Enter the garden of effacement – Look!
inside your own immortal soul: Eden
Move just a little bit ahead of Self
to see what's beyond, above the heavens –
    the monarch of fine meanings, mystic truths
    royal banners, parasols of ancient light
When that scene comes in sight, do not seek out
distinction; the distinctive miracles
of saints are just the signposts pointing here
To the sea's edge the flood is visible,
but once those waters merge, the flood will drown
    We are mated by you, Shams of Tabriz
    To you our endless pledge and greetings, mate!

* Ghazal 378

YOU, LEADER of the prayers to Love*
Let out with your "God is Great!"
for you are drunk
Shake your hands in dance
Turn your back on existence
You were promised to be on time
so you were making haste
Now that the call to prayer has come
Get moving! Don't just sit there!
Hoping for the altar of truth
you carve a hundred altars
Hoping for the love of that idol
you adore a hundred idols
Fly up a little higher,
my love, my obedient love,
for the moon's up high
and the shadow's down low
Don't bang on every door
like a door-to-door beggar
Grab the knocker of heaven's door
Since your arms are long, it's within your grasp
Since heaven's flagon's made you like this,
be stranger to the world, having freed yourself from self
I ask you how you are.
How can Howlessness be asked how are you?
Tonight you're drunk and ruined,
when tomorrow comes you'll see
How many casks you've opened
   how many glasses smashed
For every glass I've broken
My reliance was on you:
   You have mended countless kinds of breakings

* Ghazal 2933

You secret artist,
who contain within a thousand forms
beyond the moon,
beyond the bright beloved orb
You've left one rival in the dust, but filled a thousand throats with words
You've pierced one breast, but spared a hundred lives and hearts
I've gone crazy, whatever I say it's madness talking,
so hurry up, if you were privy to God's "*Am I not ...*"   [7:172]
   and say *yes, yes*

THAT REDCLOAK*
  who rose over us last year
  like the new moon
  has appeared this year
  in a rust-colored dervish coat
The Turk you saw that year
  busy with plunder
is the same who came this year
  like an Arab
It's the very same love,
  though in different garb:
  He changed clothes and appeared again
It's the same wine, though the glass has changed
  See how happy he comes in his tipsiness!
The night's gone –
  Where are my morning partners in drunken revel
  now that the torch lights up the window of mysteries?
When the Abyssinian age began, the fair Greek disappeared
Today it emerges with great hosts of battle
  Proclaim:
  the Sun of Truth of Tabriz has arrived!
  for this moon of many lights
  has climbed the wheeling skies of purity!

* Ghazal 650

IN THE END time*
there is no helper
but Salah al-Din
Salah al-Din, that's it!
If you know the secret of his secret
Don't breathe a word
so no one else finds out

A lover's breast is sweetest water
souls float on his surface
like thorn and thistle
When you see his face
do not speak
for breath obscures the mirror:
    The sun rises
        from the hearts of lovers
        the whole world shines
        fore and aft

* Ghazal 1210

BEREFT OF you both earth and sky shed tears!*
Heart adrift in blood, mind and soul in tears
because none in the world can take your place.
For you space and meta-space mourn and weep:
Gabriel, the angels, feathers blued,
the prophets and saints, eyes all ablur,
by lamentation choked, I cannot speak
to make you metaphors of how I cry.

As you left this house, fortune's roof collapsed
Now Fortune grieves for those sore-bereaved.
You proved not one man but a hundred worlds
Last night I dreamt the next world weeps for this.
All eyes fixed on you fading from our view;
Shorn of living light, these eyes wept bloody tears.
If not so proud for you, I too would burst
as my bloodied heart drips secret tears:
Cut off from you, each breath coughs blood.
Not tears, but sacks of fresh-cut musk are shed

Alas and alas and alas, alas
that doubtful hearts should weep for an eye so clear
    Salah al-Din the king, fleet phoenix, flown,
    an arrow upward sped, the bowstrings cried,
        Not just anyone can mourn Salah al-Din,
        but one who truly knows to mourn true men.

* Ghazal 2364

O LIGHT OF Truth, Hosam al-Din! Let's add*
a sheet or two, description of the *pir*.
I know your subtle body has no strength,
and yet without your sun we have no light ...
You hold our thread of thought within your hand
Your blessings string our heart with meaning's pearls.
Write down the circumstances of the *pir*
who knows the way. Choose this *pir* and let him guide!

---

* From *Masnavi* Book 1: 2934–8

SO, IN EVERY AGE, a saint arises –*
    testing continues till the Resurrection
All those of goodly character are saved
All those who have a heart like glass will break
The "living established Imam" is that saint
    Whether descended from 'Umar or 'Ali.
He, O seeker, is the Mahdi and the Guide
Whether hid or seated right before you.
He is like light and wisdom is his Gabriel
The lesser saints but lamps lit up by him.
The one who's less than these lamps is our flame.
Light emanates in grades as per a scheme,
for seven hundred veils obscure Truth's light
and all these veils of light stack up in tiers
Behind each veil there stands a certain folk –
these veils – rank after rank, till the Imam!
Those at the bottom tier, in the weakness
of their eyes, cannot bear the light above
and the next tier through the weakness of their sight
cannot stand the light of the tier above.

* From *Masnavi* Book 2: 815–24

IX

Poems of

DREAMS AND VISIONS

"I am Truth" shone from Mansur's lips like light
"I am Lord" fell from Pharoah's lips by force.
— Masnavi Book 2: 305

I saw all atoms with their mouths agape
Tell all they devour, and the tale won't end!
— Masnavi Book 3: 26

When you possess the attributes of Glory
pass like Abraham through fires of fleshly ills
and the flames will feel cool and safe to you
— Masnavi Book 3: 9–10

HOW COULD I know this melancholy*
   would make me so crazy,
make of my heart a hell
   of my two eyes raging rivers?
How could I know a torrent would
   snatch me out of nowhere away,
Toss me like a ship upon a sea of blood,
that waves would crack that ship's ribs board by board,
   tear with endless pitch and yaw each plank
that a leviathan would rear its head,
   gulp down that ocean's water,
      that such an endless ocean could dry up like a desert,
that the sea-quenching serpent could then split that desert
could jerk me of a sudden, like Korah, with the hand of wrath
     deep into a pit?

When these transmutations came about
   no trace remained of that desert or the sea
   How should I know how it all happened
   since how drowned within Howlessness?

What a multiplicity of how could I knows!
   But I *don't* know –
   for to counter that sea
   rushing in my mouth
   I swallowed a froth of opium

* Ghazal 1855

TODAY I SAW him*
   the friend
   the glow in every deed
He was gliding on the heavens like
   the soul of Mustafa
The sun before his face: ashamed
The celestial globe: latticed by stars, like my tattered heart
From his radiating splendor, water and clay beam brighter than fire

Show me a ladder, I said
so I can clamber onto the heavens

Your head is the ladder, he said
Plant your head under your heels
As you set foot on your own head
you step above the stars
Once you've staved in your lust
let your feet lift you up in the air. Come!
Up in the heavens, in the air
a hundred roads unfold before you
You'll fly over the sky
every morning
like a prayer

* Ghazal 19

O FRIEND, within whom I have disappeared!*
I dreamt I saw you in a wondrous form
Like the ladies of Egypt in their love for Joseph
I cut citrons, lost control and cut my hand
    Where has that moon gone?
    Where those eyes of last night?
    Where those ears with which I heard it all?
        Nowhere to be found:
        not you
        not me
        not that moment
        not those teeth that nipped my lips

I am a silo brimming with melancholia
    for I reaped melancholy
    after melancholy
    from that tillage

You calm the hearts of the melancholic
You are my Dhu al-Nun, my Junayd, my Bayazid!

* Ghazal 1507

102

HERE'S JOSEPH'S coat*
and the scent of him!
　He himself
　can't be far behind these two
The must of ruby wine gives joyful tidings:
After me, the goblet and the serving gourd!
　Your I-am-God soul ascends Hallâj-like
　its divine light shining ray upon ray
Stones can never harm the water
though stones can shatter jugs
Aqua Vitae
cannot be contained
within your mind;
dig a trough
for the water flows
and needs a channel
Douse with water
this jealous fire
whose winds blow
across this earth

The Love and Wisdom
of the house are
locked in strife
their screeching and screaming
echoes in the street outside
The wealth or clothes
that Love forgoes
come in the end
back to it again

* Ghazal 997

Though the groom pays
great price to his bride
her trousseau and herself
both come to him
in the end
You asked for a table from heaven
Rise up from your self and wash your hands,
it descends!
Glad tidings, love!
a new sign has come
from Shams-e Din in Tabriz

WE ARE LOVE'S FLAME that has reached the wax*
Candle-like, we've overcome the poor moth
We've made a manly, drunken charge
to forgo knowledge, and arrived at the Known

In the first stage, two leagues away from Being
We joined the caravan of a deceased community
A moon neither high nor low shined down on us
and we reached the spot where none is praised, none blamed

Let the stone-hearted and mean-spirited turn green with envy!
We attained to the presence of that ruby unbounded by time and space
Through the Throne verse we soared up to His Seat
We even saw the *Living One* and came to the *Self-subsisting*   [K2:255]

Today, how verdant and melodic that garden has made us!
So do not suppose, Sir, that we came away deprived
    Like falcons, we leave the ruins to the owls
    We are not owls, though we roost in this realm
    We've cut the pagan cincture from the Caesar of Anatolia
    Take the news to Tabriz, that we have arrived in Rome

* Ghazal 1481

I'M OUT OF my senses and you are smashed –*
who will see us home? I've told you so many times:
   don't drink so much
   just two glasses
   maybe three
I don't see a single sober soul in town
each more demented and fermented than the next

Soul of life!
   come to the ruins
   and taste the spice of life
   what savor can the spirit know
   without the converse of the soul's delight?
   How can the heart rejoice
   parted from the one who pumps it?

In every corner lies a drunk
hand on the handle of a goblet
and here's the Server who affirms our existence
with her royal chalice.
Your sustenance: in the tavern
your income and expenses: wine
Never trust a sober soul
with a single drop of sustenance

Go on, play your lute
you drunken gypsy!
Who's more sotted, you or I?
I know my magic holds no spell
cast before a drunkard such as you!

* Ghazal 2309

I left my house, a drunk came up to me
his every look was pregnant
with a hundred roses, garden bowers
Like a ship without an anchor
he wobbled left and bobbled right
every wise and careful scholar
nearly died on seeing him
I asked him: Where are you from?
   He mocked me, saying: My dear
   I'm half from Turkestan
   I'm half from Central Asia
   I'm half clay and water
   I'm half heart and spirit
   half seashore, half precious pearl
I said: Then, be my companion
for we are kith and kin!
   He replied: I do not know my kin from strangers

I am heartlorn and unturbaned
hungover in the tavern
My breast swells heavy with a weight of words –
shall I get them off my chest, or no?

   When you walk with cripples
   you have to learn to limp
   I gave you this advice before
   from the sagest source
   have you ignored it?
   What a good little sot you are –
   Are you denser than a stick of wood?
   For in the end the Moaning Pillar cried:
Sun of Truth from Tabriz!
Now that you have stirred
such ravishing revolt in motion
why do you avoid us?

I HAVE SEEN a vision, worthy of attention and praise!*
Come, Mantic of the Age, see what form my dream assumed:

In a dream I have seen the moon

What does it mean in a dream, the moon? For in dreams things
are resolved, what has come and what will come.

> That moon who lights the heart when heart feels mystery's
>   presence
> Such heart-bright sensibility spills out, illuminates the face
> *On that day* some faces *will be dawn-bright, laughing*   [K80:39]
> This was it!
> *Blessed, glad for their efforts*   [K88:9]
> So it was!

Drive off these wild beasts before they slay the mind's brain
We stuff our ears with cotton against this and that delirious rant
Just a couple breaths of life are left –
will covetous phantasma dog me to the end?!
No one is at home; do not build your house on earth

The night has passed, the dawn has come.
Get up, don't be asleep and heedless!
    – as if the rays of the sun of faith would leave you heedless!

> A horde of Tatars and armed warriors, the horizons are
>   pregnant with enmity
> Say: tear the belly of the heavens – it may give this fetus birth
> Enter the fray of brightness – how long Tatars and Armenians?
> Strap on blade, wrap on shroud, onward!
> How long worldly robe and garb?

* Ghazal 1839

On the eve of a Saturday, the fifth day of the month of Qa'da
It is six hundred and fifty, plus four more years
There is commotion in the city. What has happened?
   It's a tremor
It's the city of Medina! Now is the report amiss or true?

Pass by Medina, go beyond and see the quaking of the earth
Regard the movement of the heavens,
   their most strange manner
Look at the sea, see the leviathan, see the blue-bruised sea
See the wave – within it, the fiery whale!
See the outline of that whale, asleep –
see Jonah of the spirit, captive.
Jonah of the spirit, who ere this
was of those who praise God   [K37:143]

I'll turn the sea like wine, beyond the three dimensions
Before all this the suspended sea was limpid, free of forms
That purity did not grow turbid, our eyes are dazed
by the drops of water and mud, the stirring of the shapes of clay

The head of him whose hand
is a hand delighting in defilement
turning our wine turbid
   let's lop it off – now, strike the blow!
Why should we not recall him?
It's only just – just what he deserves.
Since enmity involves focus on a thing, heedlessness wards off enmity:

A lover once asked a fortune-teller for a written charm,
who said, take this amulet and bury it beneath the earth,
but while you bury it, do not think of monkeys,
for the thought of monkeys will distance you from your mate.
Every which way he went to plant that buried charm
a monkey's form appeared in ambush of his heart.

If only you wouldn't mention the monkey, he sighed
None who seek your help would make monkeys of their heart.
Do not needle me, he said
Do not pour salt in the wound
Put yourself to enchanting sleep

Do not go to sleep Hosam-e Din

THIS WORLD would be engulfed in flames,
    If the lover's soul would speak*
  and this rootless world would smash together like so many atoms
The world would turn to sea, the sea – in awe – into Negation
Not man, not humanity remain, though entreating Adam's kinship
Smoke arises from the spheres, neither creatures nor angels remain
and from that smoke flames soon stretch up to the majestic vault
It's then the heavens crack, neither Being nor Space remain
Chaos churns through the universe and all celebration turns lamentation
Here the water burns in fire, there the water drinks the flames
The sun falls and fails, no brighter than the spark of human soul
    Don't seek answers from the uninitiates,
      For even intimates can barely tell.
While waves of void surge over fiery comets and the dark
Mars drops its manliness, Jupiter's celestial books burn up
The moon wanes in grandeur, its joy turns to grief
Mercury sinks into mire, and Saturn goes up in flames
Venus grows pale, untuned its happy music
No bow and no rain, no wine and no chalice remain
No pleasure, no bliss, no balm salving any wound
No water to streak the plains, no winds to ripple earth
No garden to refresh and delight, no spring clouds to sprinkle, bedew
Neither pain remains nor physic, no contesting litigant, no witness
Neither flute remains nor air, not harp and not arpeggio
All causes fold away into eternity, the Saqi serves herself
Spirit chimes "My Lord on High"
Heart will go "My Lord the all-knowing"
Rise up, for the limner of eternity has set to work a second time
imprinting on the embroidered Tapestry immutable patterns
Truth has stoked its fires, so that all untruth is burned away
Fire burns the false, and the new world's heart is purely forged

* Ghazal 527

The sun of True heart stands east of it,
An east whereof constant lightning flashes
streak through the scion of the unseen
to alight upon Jesus of Mary

X

Poems about the Religion of Love

WAYS OF REASON, MODES OF LOVE

Limited Reason's like a lightning flash –
We can't go in a flash from here to Vaxsh.
The flash of lightning's not to guide your way;
But comes, instead, commanding clouds to cry
                                        – Masnavi Book 4: 3319–20

If Reason clearly saw its way along,
Fakhr-e Razi would zero in on truth.
But "he who has not tasted does not know,"
and so his fancy reason just confused him.
                                        – Masnavi Book 5: 4144–5

Whether I go east or west
or climb the sky,
there is no sign of life
until I see sign of you

I was the ascete of a country
I held the pulpit
Fate made my heart
fall in love and
follow after you

– from Ghazal 2152

Love is but blessing and fortune
Nothing but guidance and a dilated heart
Bu Hanifa never studied love
Shafi'i never related anything about it
The law of permissible and impermissible
Pertains from now until the day of death
The knowledge of lovers is eternal

– from Ghazal 499

LOVE RESIDES not in learning*
   not in knowledge
   not in pages and pamphlets
Wherever the debates of men may lead
   that is not the lovers' path

Love's branches arch over pre-eternity
   and yes, its roots delve down forever
A tree resting not on soil
   nor trunk
   nor even Heaven's throne

We deposed reason,
   punished passion with the lash –
   this reason and these morals
   were degrading to such glory

It's like this:
   So long as you long
   you idolize longing.
Become the beloved
and put an end to longing
   The incessant hopes and fears
   of the sea-faring man
   float upon planks;
   but obliterate
   both planks and seaman
   and only submersion remains

* Ghazal 395

Shams of Tabriz! the sea is you
   the pearl, too
   because your being
   head to toe
   is nothing
   but the mystery
   of the Maker

THE SEEKER of the Court of God's like this:*
When God appears, the seeker fades away
Yes, this encounter brings eternal life,
but effacement comes before undying life
Could shadows, say, be seekers of the light?
When the light shines, the shadows disappear.
How could reason live when sacrificed to Him?
All but His face shall perish from the earth   [K28:88]
Being and nothing fade before His face;
What a miracle, to be in nothingness!
In these precincts wisdom and logic fail
and at this point, the pen is split in two

* From *Masnavi* Book 3: 4658–63

YOU ATTAIN to knowledge by argument*
You attain a craft or skill by practice
If what you want is righteous poverty
that's won by *sohbat*, not by hand or tongue
The knowledge of it passes soul to soul
not by way of talk or reams of notes
Although its signs are in the seeker's heart
the seeker does not learn to read those signs
until his heart becomes exposed to light
    Then God reveals: *Did We not expose*   [K94:1]
    for We exposed the chambers of your breast
    and placed that exposition in your heart

* From *Masnavi* Book 5: 1062–7

THE EYE wants something new to see*
   and follows after that
The soul wants joy and pleasure
   and follows after that
The head wants giddiness for some new idol
   and follows after that
The legs want wearing out at the bidding of a lover
   and follow after that
Love wants to soar up to the heavens
   and follows after that
The intellect wants learning, cultivation
   and follows after that

Beyond reason's explanation there are wonders, mysteries –
the eye is veiled that only looks to causes and effect

The lover subjected in this world
   to infamy's hundred accusations
will enjoy, when it comes time for union,
   one hundred honors and distinctions
We stomach the wasteland trek, its pebbles,
   the camel's milk, marauding bedouin plunder
   for the goal of pilgrimage
Knowing the lips pleasures from a lover's luscious rubies
   the pilgrim places soulful kisses
   on the Black Stone at the Kaaba

Upon the mint of speech cast no more silver coins!
He who follows after them will find a motherlode of gold

* Ghazal 617

THE THINKER is always at pains to make his mark*
The lover always comes undone, gets all worked up
Thinkers are cautious, avoid the water's edge
Lovers make deep-sea drowning their profession
Thinkers find ease in making things easy
Lovers find leisure's bindings disgraceful
    In a gathered crowd a lover's alone
just as oil and water poured together remain apart
Do you love to reform lovers with wholesome advice?
You'll only reap passionate humiliation
    Love smells of musk
    that's how it gets a bad reputation:
    Musk always has a whiff of notoriety about it.
Love is like a tree, and lovers the shade of that tree:
    The shadows are rooted, no matter how tall they grow
To acquire reason, a child must grow old
In acquiring love, an old man grows young.
        Shams of Tabriz!
        In loving you
        the one who embraces lowliness
        will – just like your love –
        be raised and lifted up

* Ghazal 1957

LET GO ALL your scheming, lover*
let yourself go mad
   go mad
just step into the heart of fire
make yourself a moth
   a moth
Turn yourself into a stranger
raze your house down to the ground
then come stand here under one roof
   beneath the same roof
and live among the lovers.
Scrape your breast, like a plate,
clean of envy, with cascades of water
then fill up like a chalice,
   like a chalice
with the wine of love
Metamorphose purely into soul
make yourself worthy of the Soulmate
If you're going to see the drunkards
   walk tipsy
   with inebriation
Like a model
your earring pendant dangles
brushing intimate against your cheek
incline that cheek and ear
   to the Mother Pearl
   that Precious Pearl
As your spirit rises in the air
from the sweetness of our tale
efface yourself and like the lovers
   be a legend
   legendary

* Ghazal 2131

The Night of the Grave is what you are
The Night of Power is what you must become
For the power dwelling in all spirits
    be a nest
    make a home

Your thoughts go traipsing off
and drag you in their wake
With decision cut off all speculation
    be a leader
    stand in front

Desire clings, and lust locks upon the heart
become a key and turn like a tumbler
    like a tumbler

With light the Chosen One caressed
that moaning pillar
are you less than that piece of wood?
    Cry out
    be empathetic
Though Solomon has told you:
    Listen to the language of the birds
like a trap the birds fly from you
    nestle them
    and be their nest
If that gorgeous idol shows her face
fill up with her like a mirror
if she lets her silky hair down
    become her comb
    and brush her
How long two-headed like a rook?
how long a peon like a pawn?
how long go crooked like a queen?

be a master of the game
and mate
Thankfully you've given to love
many gifts and wealth
put away your money, give yourself
be gratitude
be grateful

For a while you were matter
for a while you were animal
for a while you were soul
become the soulmate
meet your soul
How long pace on the roof and vineyard?
Fly, my ratiocinating soul, into the house
Abandon all this rationalizing talk
Don't wag the jaw
don't jabber on

AMONG LOVERS don't be a wise guy*
especially with such a sweetly met love
Let the wise ones keep far away from lovers
    (the morning breeze should avoid the stench of the bathhouse sewer!)
If a wise one walks in, tell him: there's no entrée!
But if a lover enters, tell him welcome, always always welcome
By the time reason makes its plans and calculations
Love will have flown up to the seventh heaven
By the time reason finds a camel for the Hajj
Love will have climbed Mount Safa
Love came and stole over this mouth of mine
Saying:
    Ascend beyond poetry
    Climb onto the realm of Pleiades

* Ghazal 182

A MAN IN love, no matter what he says*
the smell of love wafts love-ward from his mouth
He speaks of jurisprudence, what emerges?
From mystic poverty, a sweet effulgence.
He blasphemes, the scent of faith arises.
He offers doubts, no doubt we grow more sure

* From *Masnavi* Book 1: 2880–2

THE GNOSTIC arcs constant toward the King's throne*
The ascete travels each month one day's road ...
Love has a thousand feathers and each one
soars over the throne beyond the Pleiades
The fearful ascetic charges on foot
Lovers fly lighter than lightning and air

* From *Masnavi* Book 5: 2180, 2191–2

IF WORDS made you certain that fire exists*
don't rest at the stage of certainty – Taste fire!
The cooked, alone, know Certitude itself
You want that Certitude? Step in the fire!

* From *Masnavi* Book 2: 860–1

XI

Poems

CELEBRATING UNION

He said with a smile: Go and give thanks
I'll offer you up
to celebrate the festival
I asked for whom am I the sacrifice?
and the friend said:you're mine, you're mine, all mine
— from Ghazal 2114

You've filled my life with joy like sacks of sugar
preserved me like a petaled rose, in sugar
And now today I'm seized by peals of laughter —
what joyous sounds you sprinkled in my mouth!
— Quatrain 1652

I speak of plural souls in name alone —
One soul becomes one hundred in their frames;
Just as God's single sun in heaven
shines on earth and lights a hundred walls
But all these beams of light return to one
if you remove the walls that block the sun
The walls of houses do not stand forever
and believers, then, will be as but one soul
— *Masnavi* Book 4: 415–18

MAY THE blessings which flow in all weddings*
be gathered, God, together in our wedding!
The blessings of the Night of Power,
   the month of fasting
   the festival to break the fast
the blessings of the meeting of Adam and Eve
the blessings of the meeting of Joseph and Jacob
the blessings of gazing on the paradise of all abodes
and yet another blessing which cannot be put in words:
   the fruitful scattering of joy
   of the children of the Shaykh
   and our eldest!

In companionship and happiness
   may you be like milk and honey
In union and fidelity
   just like halva and sugar.
May the blessings of those who toast
   and the one who pours the wine
   anoint the ones who said Amen and
   the one who said the prayer.

* Ghazal 236

YOU'RE A SPRIG of rose!*
From you, the garden's green and joy
Your partner in this dance, the breeze
The wind like Gabriel, you a Mary
Born to this pair: Jesus of silkrose cheeks
The dance of you two, key to the ever-life
    Endless mercy on this dance!
The throne room of your generation: the brain
The throne is the place of Kay Qobâd
The fruit of each branch finds its way
to the pit of the stomach
for they grew in a world of creation and decay
Our daily blessings, since they stem from the Creator
Do not mix with eating and somnolence
Each folk's daily bread from a different garden
    Your banquet table is most large, bountiful one!
It's apportioned by fortune. Go and seek your fortune –
    Fortune's better than furnishings, to make the story short!
Enough! A gentle breath blows through the heart-matrix
from that helping light which brings forth birth.

* Ghazal 1003

ONCE MORE we come like dust adance in air*
　　From beyond the skies of love, aturn
On the field of love like polo balls we roll
　　skittering to the side, coming to the fore

Love reduces one to need – if that's your lot
　　it suits you. Not us, who come from the beyond
This gathering's in your honor and the guests
　　have all arrived. But not for bread alone
　　we come here; pour out the firewater!
As you course through our veins, made wretched by
　　our wounds for you, thank God we come quick to life!
Shams of Truth this love of yours thirsts for my blood
　　I head straight to it, blade and shroud in hand!
Tabriz aboil, your salt alone can simmer!
　　We – pride of all the earth in caring for you –
　　have come to help you stir up the age.

* Ghazal 1720

DO NOT sleep*
   my hospitable friend, tonight
   for you are spiritous spirit
   and we are ailing ill tonight

Banish sleep from inner seeing eyes
   let mysteries appear tonight
You are the giant planet, yes
   yet revolve around this moon
   circling through the turning firmament tonight
Through the constellations you soar
   like the soul of winged Ja'far
   stalking the Eagle, Altair, as prey
To burnish separation's rust
   from the deep dark blue
   God has given you polish tonight

Praise God, all creatures have gone to sleep
   leaving me involved with my creator tonight
   What wakeful fortune, bright glory!
   I am conscious of the wakeful God tonight!
   If my eyes close shut to rest until the dawn
   I'll despise, denounce my eyes tonight

Though the market place is empty now
   Look! What commerce in the milky ways tonight
Our terrestrial night is daytime in the world of stars
   and so celestial shining fills up our view tonight
   Leo pounces on Taurus
   Mercury decks its crown with diadem
   Saturn plants surreptitious seeds of tumult
   Jupiter showers golden coins

* Ghazal 296

133

Rumi: Swallowing the Sun

I sit silent, lips shut
   and yet
I speak volumes
 without words
    tonight

TOP OF THE MORNING, you're already smashed!*
    Yes you are, you tied your turban crooked.
I swear to God, all night last night till dawn
    you were drinking – pure wine, undiluted;
It's plain in your eyes, your cheeks, your color
    the sort you are – wouldn't put it past you.
Give the tipplers some of what you tasted
    O Guardian of all created blessings

Today the lion prowls around for prey
    the vale and mountain tremble at the thought
From him you'll not escape by running!
    Submit, like head-bowed lover and you're saved.
You will live on in blissful safety
    once you are joined to his eternal realm

Run away from all this talk, run sixty leagues,
    You're at sixes and sevens in talk's trap

* Ghazal 3153

TOP OF THE MORNING, you're already smashed!*
    Oh, yes you are! You tied your turban crooked.
Today your eyes look shot, all glazed over
    I think you drank a hundred proof last night
Light of our lives and light of our hearts!
    Salutations to you! How are you feeling?
You imbibed and traveled to the heavens
    got yourself sotted and broke all bonds
    The face of reason always freezes hearts,
    The face of love turns all heads giddy
You got sotted, started wrestling lions
    wine-suckled, rode bareback on a lion's neck
Like an old shaykh the aged wine guided you
    Go now, freed from the ancient spinning wheel.

Saqi, you hold truth and justice on your side
    refusing worship to all things but wine
You've borne away our reason,
but this time carry us away
like we'll never go again

* Ghazal 3154

A LITTLE apple*
half red, half yellow
recalls a tale
of rose and saffron:

Sunder lover from beloved –
    cuteness goes with the latter
    pain falls to the former
Love reveals
two contrary colors
in one severance
on the cheeks of each:
    yellow clashes with kissable cheeks
    red and hale feel cold to lovers' cheeks
    (When the one you love plays hard to get
    don't fight it, lover, just play along).

I'm like the thorn, my lord like the rose
Though the two are in reality one
He is the sun and I, then, the shade
From him eternity's heat, from me the cold
    When Goliath came to battle Saul: [K2:247–51]
    "David, *measure the chainmail well*!"   [K34:11]

The body bears the heart
but the heart rules the body
    just as woman gives birth to man
but within the heart
another heart is hidden
like a rider in a cloud of dust
    (the knight kicks up the dust
    it's him that makes it dance)

* Ghazal 968

137

It's not like chess
   where you ponder your next move
Be reliant, like in backgammon:
   pray and cast your dice

The heart of the sun
is Shams of Tabriz
   all fruits of the heart
   bask in his warmth and grow

EXQUISITE LOVE, what exquisite love we have*   O God!
How fine, how good, how beautiful,   O God!
How warm, how warm this sun-like love keeps us –
How hidden, hidden, yet how manifest,   O God!
The moon, the exquisite moon, and exquisite wine – both here with us
adorning the spirit and the material world,   O God!
What ferment, what exquisite ferment the world stirs up
What exquisite works, what exquisite fruits they have there O God!
The king of king of knights has had a great fall, had a great fall
kicking up an exquisite dust, what exquisite dust   O God!
We've fallen, how we have fallen – never to get up again
We don't know, don't know what all this commotion is, O God?
From every lane, each and every lane: a smoke of different colors
Once more and again once more, what mad passion is this O God?
Neither trap nor fetter, so why are we in this bind?
What bonds, what fetters chain our feet   O God?!
What plans, and O what plans in the sizzling of these hearts?
It's strange, it's so strange, coming from above   O God!
Silent, you are silent, that it may not be revealed
for unknown persons hem us in left and right,   O God

* Ghazal 95

IN THIS COLD and rain*
it's better to have a lover
   A beauty at your side, love in mind
   A beauty at your side, like a picture –
   delicate and nice, supple and fresh, limpid
In this cold we rush to his neighborhood
   (none like him is born to any mother)
In this snow I'll kiss those lips of his
   (snow and sugar make the heart beat faster)
I can't stand it, I can't hold on any longer
   (they carried me off and brought me back)
When his image suddenly lights up the heart
The heart just runs from its place, God is great!

* Ghazal 1047

BLISS –*
  the instant
    spent seated
      on the terrace,
        me next to you
          two forms and
          two faces
            with just one soul,
              me and you

The chatter of birds
the garden's murmur
flowing like a fountain of youth
as we stroll through roses,
        me and you
The stars of the firmament, bent low to look over us
Let's eclipse them, shine like the moon,
        me and you

        Me and you join,
beyond Me
beyond You
in joy
happy, released from delire and delusion
        Me and you, laughing like this,
reach dimensions where celestial birds suck sugary cubes
    Magical! Me and you, here,
in our corner of earth,
but wafting on airs of Iraq and Khorasan,
        me and you

* Ghazal 2214

In one form here on earth
in other forms in paradise,
eternal, sunk in fields of sugar,
                me and you

XII

Poems of

DEATH AND BEYOND

Shams-e Tabriz is gone and who
will weep for the best among men?
The world of meaning's gained in him a bride,
but shorn of him the world of forms just weeps
                                        – from Ghazal 2893

You who fly from this narrow cage
veering off beyond the heavens
You'll see a new life after this
how long will you bear this life's drear? ...
This body wore a butler's garb
  now sports more fashionable form
   Death means life and this life is death
   though heathen eyes see negative
All souls departed from this body
live on, but hidden now, like angels ...
When body's bricks crumble, don't wail
Sir, you've been only in a jail
When you emerge from jail or pit,
you stand regal, tall, like Joseph

                                        – from Ghazal 3172

> *On the day I die*
> *as they bear along my bier*
> *do not suppose*
> *I'm chagrined at losing this world.*
> *Don't cry for me and do not lament*
>
> — from Ghazal 911

> *The human frame: a talisman made quick*
> *an essence pure now kneaded in the clay*
> *When heaven breaks that talisman apart*
> *to clay returns the clay, to Pure the pure.*
>
> — Quatrain 1067

WHERE HAVE you gone*
   you godly martyrs?
   you seekers of calamity
   on the hot plain of Karbala?
Where have you gone
   soaring souls, lovers lofted up
   above the birds of heaven?
Where have you gone
   monarchs of the skies
   discoverers of a portal
   to pass through the firmament
Where have you gone
   all disencumbered
   of person and place?
One demands that reason answer:
Where are you?
Where are you
   who smashed in the jailer's door
   who freed the debtors from the prison
Where are you
   who opened the treasury
Where are you
   melody without sound?

You dove into that Sea
   of which this earth is only foam
   We can still make you out, for a moment more
   Sea-foam : the forms of the world
   pass beyond foam
   if your essence is clarity, pure

* Ghazal 2707

My heart froths up
   with the image of these words
Give up the image
delve into the heart, if you belong to us

   Rise up
   Sun of Tabriz
   from the East
   for you are
   the essence of the essence of the essence of light

YOU FLEW OFF in the end –*
   verged into the hidden
But how? How – by what road
   did you depart the world?
Oh, your feathers fluttered
   your wings beat – broke the cage
and you took to the air
   soaring toward the soul world

A royal falcon you were
   caught in the Old Hag's jess
The falcon-drum called you back
   to the Placeless perch
Intoxicated, you –
   a nightingale among
   the inauspicious owls
   When it came over you –
   the rose bower's fragrance –
you flew toward the hand of
   the one who plucks the rose

This sour yeast's sore yield:
A throbbing hangover
But in the end you found
Eternity's tavern
Straight as an arrow speeds
   you marked fortune's target
   You whizzed toward that target
   Fleeing this tautly bowed arch

The crooked world, ghoul-like
misled you here to there

* Ghazal 3051

You passed beyond those signs
   heading toward the Traceless
What to do with that crown
   now that you are a sun
   or with this regal belt?
What good these, to a head
   disappeared from our midst?

I've heard that with both dead eyes
   we'll stare up at the soul
Why do you gaze soul-ward
   who've joined with the soul of Soul.
O heart, what a rare bird!
   in hunting your reward
   You flew forward toward spears
   held up both wings for shields
Roses shrink from autumn
   But you're a bold-bud rose
   braving fall blasts, you went –
   not all in one fell swoop –
   but skittering slowly

From heaven to the earth
You poured down on the roof
and like the raindrops ran
every which-way, to learn
the drainpipe spits you out

   Silence! Enough talk – sleep!
   You've sheltered with the Friend

AND NOW IT'S time*
    for love's union
    for God's vision
    for resurrection, everlasting life
Time for grace, for blessing
    for surging pure oceans of purity
    the sea foams white, casts its treasures:
    Fortunate dawn, morn of the light of God!
    Whose face? What image? King or prince?
    What ancient sage is this?
All these are only veils
fervid ardor burns these veils away
You have the mind's eye to taste him
You writhe for it in your head
but you are all of two minds
    an earthly head of clay
    and one celestial, pure
All these celestial heads
lay scattered in the dust
to show you that another mind's afoot
At root, essential mind is hidden
and only branches dangle to our eyes
Know that beyond this universe
another endless world awaits
    Seal up the skin, my host,
    no vintage can convey us there
    The jug of apprehension's bottlenecked in those straits

The Sun of Truth shone from Tabriz
    and I told him:
    Your light touches all
    and yet remains apart

* Ghazal 464

149

I DIED TO mineral, joined the realm of plants*
I died to vegetable, joined animal
I died from animal to human realm
So why fear? When has dying made me less?
In turn again I'll die from human form
only to sprout an angel's head and wings
and then from angel-form I will ebb away
For *All things perish but the face of God*   [K28:88]
And once I'm sacrificed from angel form
I'm what imagination can't contain.
So let me be naught! Naughtness, like an organ,
sings to me: *We verily return to Him*   [K2:151]
Know that death – the community's agreed –
is like the fount of life in darkness hid

*From *Masnavi* Book 3: 3901–7

XIII

Poems about

BIRTHING THE SOUL

The lady of my thoughts gives constant birth
She's pregnant but with the light of your glory

— from Ghazal 2234

Shams al-Haqq of Tabriz, my heart's pregnant with you
when will I see a child born by your fortune

— from Ghazal 2331

You are my sky, I am the earth, dumbfounded:
what things you sprout from my heart each moment!
I'm parched earth, rain down on me drops of grace,
for your water makes the earth grow rosy
What does the earth know what you sow in it?
you made it pregnant, you know what it bears
every atom pregnant with your mysteries —
you make it writhe a while in pangs of birth
What marvels writhe to birth through the world-womb:
An "I am God," the call "Glory to me"

— from Ghazal 3048

Before I wanted an audience to buy what I said
Now I only want you to ransom me from my words
I carved many an idol to deceive the folk
Now I am drunk on the Abrahamic friend
and am sick of the carver of idols
A colorless imperceptible idol
distracted my handiwork:
"Go find another master
for the gallery of idols"
I've sold the studio
put aside suppositions
learned the value of madness
purified myself of speculations
When some form comes before my eyes
I yell at my heart: Get out, deceiver!
and if it hesitates at all,
I raze its foundations …

– from Ghazal 2449

HEART,*
sit at the foot of one who knows his hearts
rest beneath the tree whose boughs bud fresh
Don't wander all around the market of perfumes
sit in the stall of him who has a stash of sugar
You'll be fleeced by every seller –
Without a scale to take their measure
you'll mistake the gilded slug for golden tender
They'll make you sit inside the shop
sweetly promising "Just one moment, please"
Don't sit there waiting,
there's another door goes out the back
Don't wait with bowl in hand for every pot to boil
what stews in every pot is not the same.
Not every cane-cut pen drips with sugar
not every under has above
not every eye's possessed of vision
not every sea conceals a pearl

Sing your little heart out, nightingale
for your famed intoxicated lamentation
echoes and transmutes the stony hills and granite boulders
If your head cannot contain you – lose it
you can't pass through the needle's eye a knotty thread
The awakened heart's a lamp
cloak it from contrary airs beneath your mantle
for the windy air will do it harm.
Pass beyond the winds and reach the spring
become a secret confidant, welling with emotion
    and then like a green tree you will swell with sap
    and come to fruition as it courses through your heart

* Ghazal 563

HERE I COME again*
again I come from the Friend
Look at me, look at me
I've come to look after you
I come in joy, rejoiced
I come freed from all

    Several thousand years went by
    before I found the words:
I ascend, ascend
I dwelt up there, am heading there
Let me go again, again
    I am at a loss here:
I was a divine bird
    see now how worldly mired I am
    I didn't see the trap
    and suddenly
    came up caught in it

I am pure light, my son
not just a fistful of clay
The shell is not me
I came as the royal pearl within

Look at me
    not with outward eye
    but with inward heart;
Follow me there and see
how unencumbered we become

* Ghazal 1390

I am
    above the four mothers
and I am
    above the seven fathers
I am
    the lodestar jewel
    come from the ore
    to be revealed

My beloved struts through the bazaar
    discerning, quick
to buy me out
or else what business
could I have at all
to be on the market
    – I come in search of him.

Shams-e Tabriz
    Won't you search me out,
    comb the earth, end to end?
    for I have criss-crossed
heart-sore
    and soul-sick
through the sands
    of effacement

BEFORE THE candle*
    that lights   the soul
                                 the heart

    is like a moth
    In the flickering
    flame
    of the beloved   the heart
    makes itself a home
A towering figure
    lion-taming
    drunk on love
    a revolution
    in the beloved's presence,
    sober,   on his own
    a madman
    the shape of anger
    the soul of peace
    a bitter face of sugar
I've never seen in all the world such a sanguine stranger

A reservoir of rational insight
when he watches the candle
his feathers shrivel to his feet
he staggers like a drunkard
    The crops in flames
    on the outstretched plains of love
fiery: his wheat
a goblet: his soul.

Light would soak the world entire
as once it did on Sinai's Mount
if I reveal the ecstasy
of my heart's fabliaux:

* Ghazal 2789

Shall I call him candle,
picture of love,
heart-stealer,
life-sustainer,
pure spirit,
tall-statured,
infidel,
soul's beloved?

An old man stomping before his dais like a drunk –
but a sea of knowledge, a philosopher and sage
holding to the hem of knowledge with his teeth
but the smith's tongs of love
    having left him not a single tooth ...
There I am, transfixed by this sage's light,
the old man completely absorbed in the beloved
He like a mirror's face, pure reflection
    I, two-headed, like a comb
I grew old in that subtle old man's beauteous glory
I like a moth in him, he having in me a moth

I finally called out:
    Master of all beings in knowledge
    and of all the climes in art,
    grant us from your grace a small abode

He said:
    You are farsighted, but closed of eye –
    I'll tell you. Heed this, the sure and
    august counsel of my heart:
    My knowledge and knowing,
    sagesse and wisdom and culture
    see how all of it is drowned

in the beauty
   of one rosy-cheeked
   and priceless pearl

When I looked, what did I see –
   the ruin of the heart and soul
O Muslims, have mercy! O Lord, some aid and succor!

   You cloak these words in mystery; say it plain!
   Do not fear the jealous, tell true and bravely – who was it?
That Tabrizi Sun of Truth and Faith, that Lord
who turned this laggard by his love into a leader!

OH, HOW colorless*
   and formless
   I am!
When will I ever see the am that I am?

You said:
   The secrets that you know, bring forth, put out, talk up!

Where is up
   or forth
   within this middle
   that I am?
When will my soul be still?
   It moves when motionless,
   the anima I am.
My sea has drowned within itself;
   what a strange and shoreless sea
   I am!

Not in this world
not in the next should you seek me out;
   both this and that have vanished
   in the world I am.
Like non-existence
   nothing profits me
   and nothing harms –
What a wondrous useless-harmless thing
I am!

I said
   Friend, you are just like me!

* Ghazal 1759

He said
    How can you speak of likeness to
    the obviousness I am?
I said
    That's it, that's what you are!
He said
    Silence! No tongue has ever uttered
    what I am.
I said
    Since no tongue has given voice to you,
    Here I am! your unutterable exposition.
    In annihilation
    I became
    inconstant
    like the moon
Now here I am! your sure-footed, footless runner.

A call arose:
    Why do you run?
    Look to see how manifestly hidden
    that I am

When I saw Shams-e Tabriz
    I became.
Now what a wondrous treasure-mine
    and sea of pearls I am!

IT'S WAVES OF LOVE that make the heavens turn*
Without that love the universe would freeze:
  no mineral absorbed by vegetable
  no growing thing consumed by animal
  no sacrifice of anima for Him
  who inspired Mary with His pregnant breath
  Like ice, all of them unmoved, frozen stiff
  No vibrant molecules in swarms of motion
Lovers of perfection, every atom
turns sapling-like to face the sun and grow
Their haste to shed their fleshly form for soul
sings out an orison of praise to God

* From *Masnavi* Book 5: 3854–9

WITH EACH NEW BREATH the sound of love*
surrounds us all from right and left
Now up we go, head heavenward
who wants to come and see the sights?
We've been before in heaven's realm
The angels there our constant friends
We'll go again
for we were born
all in that town.

We are ourselves above the skies
a greater host than angels there;
why should we not exceed their rank
since our abode is Majesty?
The purest pearl
does not belong
in earthly dust.

What brought you down? What place is this? Pack up!

By fortune blessed to give our lives,
the caravan will guide our steps:

> Our pride in life, the Chosen One
> By His bright orb the moon was split
> (it would not turn its gaze away)
> And so luck smiled upon the moon
> the lowly moon that begs its light!
> The wind's sweet scent drips from his locks
> His image shines with brilliant rays
> from his bright face, reflecting from
> *And the sun in its zenith*   [K 93:1]

See how my heart with every beat
reveals the moon cleft clear in two
    why do you turn your sight down from such a sight?

* Ghazal 463

Like water birds, man's born within
the sea of soul
How could he nest within the mire,
that ocean bird?
And we are all pearls in that sea,
afloat on it,
or else why wave on wave would surge
all through our hearts?
Over our boat just like a wave
broke *Am I not*   [K7:172]
Our ship's ribs staved, the boat will sink
our time has come for reunion,
to meet with God.

INFUSE OUR veins with love's aqua vitae*
show us dark nocturne reflections
of the morning's draught
Father of fresh joys, course quick through our veins!
Like the magic grail
brim up both worlds, reveal the heavens
You who stalk my wits
who live by firing arrows
pinch my heartfeathers taut on to your string
raise your arms and take my life as target

> If reason's watchman blocks your path and plan
> Strategize, devise excuse, escape him
> Is it proverbial "Red of complexion, short of magnanimity"?
> See the magnanimity in ruddy wine, and make it legendary
> The stars have played you like a pawn –
> made you march about, checkmated you
> Choose a knight, storm the castle, charge the king
> Get up, set your cap askance, avoid all traps
> Kiss the cheeks of spirit, comb the locks of joy
> Climb the heavens, get acquainted with the angels
> Reach the *court of righteousness*   [K54:55]
> and bow in service to its threshold

Once his dreamy image makes your heart its haunt
Dwell phantomlike in heart and mind:
you'll see two tubs,
one full of fire and one of gold
choose the fire and plunge your hand right in
Be like him who spoke with God:
> Do not covet the golden tub

* Ghazal 1821

Take the fire into your mouth
turn the land into a tongue of fire
Tame the feral lions
make enemies your intimates
Call the foe's blood Magian wine

Come, saqi!
   We call on you to ward away dualities
   Put one strong shot in my palm
   and unite all multiplicities in one

It's true, this home, our world,
extends in six directions
yet just one point will orient us
since that focal point of adoration
has no homeland,
build your nest in nothingness
Time's a relicker, wearing all things out
for immortality don't look to it.
Everlasting life's above, beyond time's span
You are what's winnowed: the wheat
the body's so much straw
   unless you're an ass
   you don't munch on straw
   Pick the meat and kernel

   The word is out
   why knock on the door?
   Knock down the door
      by your spirit
   set out for the psyche

NOTES ON THE POEMS

The notes provided here are offered where some explanation was felt essential to the understanding of the poem for non-specialists; they are not intended as a systematic commentary or as literary analysis. Indeed, some ghazals did not seem particularly in need of notes at all, and most of the *Masnavi* passages explain themselves. Quotations from or allusions to passages from the Koran (*Qur'ān*) are indicated in brackets on the right-hand side of the page.

I. ORISONS TO THE SUN: POEMS OF PRAISE AND INVOCATION

The poem fragments that begin this section are addressed to Shams-e Tabrizi, or Shams al-Din of Tabriz, the figure who transformed Rumi's spiritual life. Shams means "sun," which name Rumi plays with frequently. Shams al-Din (Sun of the Faith) and Shams al-Haqq (Sun of Truth) are also titles Rumi uses for Shams.

SUDDEN RESURRECTION! Endless Mercy!   Ghazal 1
Ay rastakhiz-e nâgahân v-ay rahmat-e bi-montahâ
Rajaz: | ⁻ ˘ ˘ ⁻ | ⁻ ˘ ˘ ⁻ | ⁻ ˘ ˘ ⁻ | ⁻ ˘ ˘ ⁻ ||

A poet's collected lyrical poems, called by the generic title *Divân* in Persian, were commonly arranged in alphabetical order, by the last letter of the line, from about the time of Rumi onward. Rumi's collection of poetry (known as the *Divân-e kabir* = the Great Divan; or *Divân-e Shams* = the Divan of Shams) is traditionally organized not strictly by alphabetical order, but also by meter. Whether by design or not, Rumi's *Divân* opens with a poem addressed to the spiritual beloved, one may assume Shams, as "Sudden

Resurrection." The poem of course ends with the Saqi, or spiritual cupbearer, pouring out the mystical experience that cannot be expressed and does not admit rational explanation.

"Angel Eyes" from the Koran describe the beauties in the symbolic paradise that awaits believers (see Koran 52:20, 56:22 and 44:54). The multichrome design may refer to Rumi's notion of the prismatic nature of reality: truth is unichrome, white light, but as it is refracted into the phenomenal world, things that are actually one appear in duality and distinction, so that even Moses may come into conflict with a Moses (see *Masnavi* Book 1: 2467). The speaking persona of the poem asks the guide/beloved for attention, which includes the reprimands of boxing his ears, but as long as exclusive attention is given to the disciple/lover, this is enough, even if the reprimands prove overwhelming and unending. Of course, the discussion is jocular in tone, and everyday events intrude on the poem, such as the bread and greens (it is worth noting that novitiates desiring entrance into the Mevlevi Order of Whirling Dervishes in later centuries had to first serve in the kitchen for 1001 days).

O MOUTHPIECE of God   Ghazal 1310
Ay nâteq-e elâhi v-ay dide-ye haqâyeq
Mozâre' akhrab al-sadrayn: | ‾ ˘ ˘ | ‾ ˘ ‾ ‾ | ‾ ‾ ˘ | ‾ ˘ ‾ ‾ ||

LOOK AT that face   Ghazal 5
Ân shekl bin v-ân shive bin v-ân qadd o khadd o dast o pâ
Rajaz: | ‾ ‾ ˘ ‾ | ‾ ‾ ˘ ˘ | ‾ ‾ ˘ ‾ | ‾ ‾ ˘ ‾ ||

"Agiary": a word used in South Asian English for a Zoroastrian fire-temple (Persian: *âtash-kade*). Zoroastrians revere fire as a symbol of beneficent force in the cosmos, but ill-informed or inimical outsiders have accused them of being "fire-worshippers." Rumi's allusion here therefore appears quite sophisticated, understanding the divine beloved as having taken on human form, a form that becomes the focal point of worship. The beauty of this godly youth overpowers the beholder and steals away his heart, as a bandit might swoop down on a caravan and plunder it. The speaking persona in the poem appeals to this godly incarnation for respite.

"Good sir" (*fatâ*): a young man, perhaps even a member of the chivalric order of young men (or *fotovvat*). The word connotes a young warrior, a knight, who has power to plunder but operates according to a code of chivalry.

"The Sun *in the Zenith*" (Shams *al-ḍuḥá*) uses a description from the opening words of Sura 93 of the Koran to apply to Shams, which of course also means "the sun".

"Come and get it" (*salá*): the call to begin eating.

Narcissi and hyacinth: the beloved's eyes are often compared to the narcissus in Persian poetry, and the facial hair of the beloved, here eyebrows, to the fragrant, bushy hyacinth.

WHAT A BANNER, what a standard   Ghazal 2407
Zahi levâ va 'alam lâ elâha ella llâh
Mojtass: | ˘ - ˘ - | ˘ ˘ - - | ˘ - ˘ - | ˘ ˘ - ||

The refrain of this poem, "there is no God but God," is of course a liturgical phrase from the obligatory prayers, repeated five times daily. It often occurs in Sufi chanting (*dhikr*) and meditation, as well.

II. POEMS OF FAITH AND OBSERVANCE

In the lines with which this chapter opens, the *mi'râj* refers to the Prophet's miraculous ascension to heaven and entrance into the luminous presence of the divine. The story is provided in suggestive outline in the Koran (53:5–18), but it was much elaborated in the Hadith, and the genre known as "stories of the prophets." The Prophet was borne aloft by a winged equine-like creature, named Burâq. Various Sufis have suggested that the fully self-realized spiritual person can repeat this journey for himself.

"Zoroast" is a poetic license, a metrical shortening of "Zoroastrian." The Persian word used here (*gabr* – sometimes rendered into English in British India as "guebre") was in quite common usage among medieval Persian Muslims as an unflattering term to denote Zoroastrians. The word used here for "Jew" (*jahud*) is also now considered derogatory, though the extent to which Rumi uses it in a necessarily derogatory sense is open to interpretation. The Koran generally uses *al-yahûd* to designate the Jews, or *Banî Isrâ'îl* for "the children of Israel." Rumi uses both *yahud* and *jahud*, which are of course etymologically related. Both *gabr* and *jahud* are now considered derogatory, though one may quibble about the emotional overtones they would have carried in the Persian verse of Rumi's time. Note, however, that in the shorthand used by Rumi and other Muslims of his day, a true "believer" (*mo'men*) is, of necessity, a Muslim. The Jews and Zoroastrians and Christians (who were also referred to with a colloquial term, *tarsâ*, less flattering in its connotations than the words appearing in the Koran) were not conceived as infidels or unbelievers in a theological sense, but rather as "People of the Book;" nevertheless, they were commonly assumed by Muslims to possess a less complete realization of revealed truth, which attitude is often implicit in the vocabulary.

FLEE TO God's Koran, take refuge in it

From *Masnavi* Book 1: 1537–44

SWEEP ALL AWAY with the broom of "No"!　　　Verses from Rumi's
Seven Sermons

THE MOTHER of fasting　　　　　　　　　　　　　　Ghazal 2375
Suye atfâl bi-âmad be-karam mâdar-e ruze
Ramal makhbun: | ˉ ˘ ˗ ˗ | ˘ ˘ ˗ ˗ | ˘ ˘ ˗ ˗ | ˘ ˘ ˗ ˗ ||

The month of Ramadan is, of course, a month of fasting for Muslims. The eastern Iranian traditions of asceticism and mysticism included additional periods of fasting, and one of Rumi's teachers, Borhân al-Din Mohaqqeq of Termez, was particularly fond of this practice.

Isaac: the Koran does not mention the name of the son Abraham was called upon to sacrifice, and in many Muslim sources it is Ishmael. Rumi seems ambivalent about which son it was, citing sometimes Isaac, sometimes Ishmael. See John Renard, *All the King's Falcons: Rumi on Prophets and Revelation* (Albany: State University of New York Press, 1994), 49–50.

CLOSE YOUR mouth to bread – here comes the sugar of the fast

Ghazal 2307

Bar band dahân az nân k-âmad shekar-e ruze
Hazaj akhrab: | ˉ ˗ ˘ | ˘ ˗ ˗ ˗ | ˉ ˗ ˘ | ˘ ˗ ˗ ˗ ||

Zamzam is the well in the sacred precincts of the Kaaba in Mecca, said to have been dug by Abraham. Pilgrims consider the water blessed and possessed of curative powers.

"Châdor": literally "tent," but also the full-length cloth that urban women in Iran use to cover their hair and bodies when in the presence of men to whom they have no blood or marriage ties.

MOSES SAW a shepherd on the road
Moses, peace be upon him, and his rejection of the shepherd's prayer
Masnavi Book 2: 1720–60 (following the Este'lâmi edition, lines 1724–64)

The story continues after the point where this passage ends with further reproach of Moses. God transforms Moses' heart with mystic knowledge. Moses chases into the desert after the shepherd and tells him not to worry about the rules of religion, but to worship with the heart. "Your blasphemy is true religion. You are saved and have saved the world." But Moses' reproach of him has also purified the shepherd and given him superior insight.

The story contains Rumi's explanation of the meaning of a Hadith, or tradition from the Prophet: "My servant is Me, and I am him." On the Day of Resurrection, God will say to his servants, "I was ill and you did not come to visit me." The servant will reply, "But you have no body, how could I visit you?" God will answer that visiting people who are sick is, in effect, a visitation of God.

Fätima: the name of the daughter of the Prophet, and a common girl's name in the Muslim world.

THE LORD, at dawn, saw need to take a bath
* *Story of a lord and his prayer-loving slave, whose communion with God in prayer and supplication was most mighty.*
Masnavi Book 3: 3055–76

AN APE can mimic man in all he does   From *Masnavi* Book 1: 282–90

WHEN SOLOMON'S royal pavilion was pitched
The Story of the Hoopoe and Solomon in explanation of "When destiny intervenes the seeing eye is closed"
Masnavi Book 1: 1202–33 (following the Este'lâmi edition, lines 1210–42)

There is a pun in this story, insofar as the Persian word for raven (*zâgh*) is the same as the Arabic verb in the Koran for "swerve" or misperceive, which comes in Surat al-Najm (53:17), speaking of Muhammad's vision of the divine presence at the lote-tree beyond which no one may approach closer to God, which he saw on the *mi'râj*: "His eye did not swerve." Thus we have "raven" (*zâgh*) and "it did not swerve" (*mâ zâgh*), which could also be interpreted as "not-raven."

ONCE THERE was this grocer with his parrot
**The tale of the grocer and his parrot and the spilling of the oil*
Masnavi Book 1: 247–65 (following the Este'lâmi edition, lines 248–66)

PILGRIMS ON THE WAY! where are you   · Ghazal 648
Ay qowm-e be hajj rafte kojâ'id kojâ'id
Hazaj akhrab makfuf: | ‾ ˘ ˘ | ˘ ‾ ˘ ˘ | ˘ ‾ ˘ ˘ | ˘ ‾ ˘ ||

The Sufi tradition of poetry often suggests that the ritual of pilgrimage has an interior meaning that can be achieved without actual performance of the outward forms, whereas the ritual might be performed without the meaning be achieved.

    In Mecca, the pilgrims circumambulate the Kaaba, a square structure that housed the idols of the Arabian tribes before the advent of Islam, but is now called "the House of God."

AS I ENTER the solitude of prayer   From *Masnavi* Book 3: 2400–4

III. POEMS OF POETRY AND MUSIC

Legend holds that Rumi did not compose poetry until the arrival of Shams in 1244, nor did he perform the related activity of *samâ'*, literally "audition." *Samâ'* involved listening to poetry accompanied by music, which sometimes moved the hearer to meditative or even ecstatic motion, akin to dance. Islamic scholars and Sufis were divided over the propriety of this action, since dance, especially as practiced at the royal courts, was generally accompanied by wine and salacious intent. Most Sufis eventually accepted the practice of *samâ'* for those people who found it aroused only their spiritual inclinations. The particular kind of *samâ'*, or "turning," performed by the Mevlevis who followed Rumi has given them the nickname of "the Whirling Dervishes."

    For an explanation of the rebec (*rabâb*), see Ghazal 304, below ("Do you get what the rebec is saying").

BY GOD, who was from pre-eternity Ghazal 1760
Be khodâ'i ke dar azal bud-ast
Khafif mahzuf: | ⏓ ˘ – – | ˘ – ˘ – | ⏑⏑ – ||

Samâ': see above, under III. Poems of Poetry and Music. This poem asserts that in the (first) absence of Shams, Rumi did not write ghazals or perform *samâ'*.

One of the rituals of the pilgrimage is stoning the pillars of Satan.

Syria, Armenia and Byzantium were geographical territories or political entities surrounding Muslim Anatolia.

LOOK AT me Ghazal 2077
Be man negar be do rokhsâr-e za'farâni-ye man
Mojtass: | ˘ – ˘ – | ˘ ˘ – – | ˘ – ˘ – | ˘ ˘ – ||

MY SUN and moon has come, my ears and eyes have come Ghazal 633
Shams o qamar-am âmad sam' o basar-am âmad
Hazaj akhrab al-sadrayn: | – – ˘ | ˘ – – (–) | – – ˘ | ˘ – – – ||

Joseph is the prophet, famous for his beauty. Solomon's ring, or seal, gives him control over the jinn and comprehension of the language of the birds. For Rumi's use of Joseph and Solomon, respectively, see John Renard, *All the King's Falcon's: Rumi on Prophets and Revelation* (Albany: State University of New York Press, 1994), 59–66 and Taqi Purnâmdâriân, *Dâstân-e payâmbarân dar Kolliyât-e Shams*, v. 1 (Tehran: Mo'assese-ye Motâle'ât va Tahqiqât-e Farhangi, 1985), 345–404.

LISTEN TO this reed "*Song of the Reed*" *Masnavi* Book 1: 1–34

"Singing legends of love's mad obsessions": Specifically, the legends of Majnun, who was touched by his unrequited love for Layla.

DO YOU get what the rebec is saying Ghazal 304
Hich mi-dâni che mi-guyad rabâb
Ramal mahzuf: | – ˘ – – | – ˘ – – | – ˘ – ||

A story is told by the hagiographer Aflâki (*Manâqeb*, 165–8) in *The Feats of the Knowers of God*, tr. John O'Kane (Leiden: Brill, 2002), 115–17, that this poem was composed in response to some Islamic legal scholars who wanted to condemn and forbid the playing of the *rabâb*. Rumi's reply, including this poem, is said to have shamed them into silence.

"Rebec": Literally, *rabâb* (or *robâb*), a kind of string instrument known for its plaintive sound. It was played with a bow, had a sound chamber covered by animal skin, and evolved in Europe into the Rebec.

"From conception to the full of youth": Compare *Masnavi* Book 3: 3901 and 4: 3637, as well as Koran 23:13.

"The spiked fiddle's strings": Literally, the *kamânche*.

"If I humor him, it will only make more thistles for him": The allusion here is somewhat obscure, and unaccounted for by Aflâki's anecdote. It may be an allusion to the dynamics of the relationship between Rumi and the Seljuq ruler, or Mo'in al-Din Parvâne. An owl is inauspicious, said to reside only in ruins. The Koranic verse that follows apparently refers to a situation of war between the believers (Muslims) and unbelievers (*alladhīna kafarū*), in which the believers are called upon to smite the unbelievers on the neck until they are overcome and taken prisoner. Then, they should either be set free or ransomed by the end of the war. God could have accomplished this punishment, but tries some servants by means of others. Those who are slain in the path of God, He will not let their deeds be in vain.

THE SEA OF HONEY sent word to me this morning   Ghazal 1357
Payâm kard marâ bâmdâd bahr-e 'asal
Mojtass: | ˇ ˘ ˇ ˘ | ˇ ˇ ˘ ˘ | ˇ ˘ ˇ ˘ | ˘ ˘ ˘ ||

Samâ' : see under Poems of Poetry and Music, *Be khodâ'i ke dar azal bud-ast*, Ghazal 1760 ("By God, who was from pre-eternity").

"Water says: you've grown from me, you'll come to me": Possibly alluding to Koran 21:30, which indicates that all life comes from water.

THEY DANCE, parade about the battlefield
From *Masnavi* Book 3: 96–100

IV. POEMS OF SILENCE

In the excerpt from the *Masnavi* on the title page of this chapter, two verses from the Koran are referenced.

"Were the sea ink for my Lord" comes from Koran 18:109: *Say: If the sea were ink for the words of my Lord, the sea would surely run dry before the words of my Lord run dry, even if another were linked to it for us.*

"Cut down all the gardens, groves for pens": This alludes to Koran 31:27: *Were all the trees on earth pens and the ocean, swelled by the seven seas beyond it, yet would the words of God not be exhausted. Verily, God is Mighty, Wise.*

I SERVE THAT orb in heaven, say no word but Orb   Ghazal 2219
Man gholâm-e qamar-am ghayr-e qamar hich ma-gu
Ramal makhbun: | ˉ ˇ ˉ ˉ | ˇ ˇ ˉ ˉ | ˇ ˇ ˉ ˉ | ˇ ˇ ˉ ||

"Orb": Literally, the moon (*qamar, mâh*), which is a metaphor for the bright face of the beloved, which totally dominates the night sky, and alongside which all other thoughts and images pale. Unfortunately, "moon face" does not carry the same positive associations in English.

MUSICIAN, FACE moonrise bright   Ghazal 2245
Motreb-e mahtâb-ru ânche shenidi be-gu
Monsareh matvi maksuf: | ˉ ˇ ˇ ˉ | ˉ ˇ ˉ | ˉ ˇ ˇ ˉ | ˉ ˇ ˉ ||

THIS HOUSE where the lute strings constantly strum   Ghazal 332
In khâne ke payvaste dar u bâng o chaghâna-st
Hazaj akhrab makfuf: | ˉ ˉ ˇ | ˇ ˉ ˉ ˇ | ˇ ˉ ˉ ˇ | ˇ ˉ ˉ ||

I CALL UPON you   Ghazal 116
Ay sakht gerefte jâdovi râ
Hazaj akhrab maqbuz: | ˉ ˉ ˇ | ˇ ˉ ˉ ˉ | ˇ ˉ ˉ ||

The raids that conquered India in the name of Muslim rulers were carried out mostly by the Turkish dynasty of the Ghaznavids. Turks earned a reputation as brave fighters, first as slaves, in which capacity they formed the royal guard of the caliph; then as the rulers of eastern Iran, under the

Ghaznavids and Seljuqs. The beloved is not infrequently compared to a young Turkish warrior-prince who slays suitors right and left with his haughty charms. On the other hand, the work of sorcery is generally considered a shamanistic, pagan and non-Islamic activity.

"Tongue of meaning" refers to the true inner meaning, as opposed to superficial understanding. "Meaning" here is *ma'navi*, the same word used in the title of the *Masnavi-ye ma'navi* – "the couplets of true meaning."

"Divine decree" (*qazâ*) and "destiny" (*taqdir*) are terms from a theological crux in Islam, which the *Masnavi* repeatedly addresses, including in the conversation between Solomon and the Hoopoe, in this collection (Poems of Faith and Observance, *The Story of the Hoopoe and Solomon*).

WHEN THE SUN came out   Ghazal 2408
Cho âftâb bar âmad ze qa'r-e âb-e siâh
Mojtass: | ˘ ‒ ˘ ‒ | ˘ ˘ ‒ ‒ | ˘ ‒ ˘ ‒ | ˘ ˘ ‒ ||

The allusions are to Joseph and Solomon. The story of Joseph, cast in the well by his brothers, only to rise out of it again, reborn, and assume in due course the kingship of Egypt, is related in Sura 12 of the Koran. The story of Solomon and the ants occurs in Koran 27:18–19. As noted previously, Rumi's prophetology respecting Joseph and Solomon is discussed in, respectively, John Renard, *All the King's Falcon's: Rumi on Prophets and Revelation* (Albany: State University of New York Press, 1994), 59–66 and Taqi Purnâmdâriân, *Dâstân-e payâmbarân dar Kolliyât-e Shams*, v. 1 (Tehran: Mo'assese-ye Motâle'ât va Tahqiqât-e Farhangi, 1985), 345–404.

"Tailor cuts the cloth": Rumi uses this metaphor elsewhere to illustrate the limits of reason. Reason is useful in that it brings you to the tailor when you have need for a new tunic, but once you get there you must turn yourself over to the hands of the tailor and let him do his work. See *Ketâb-e Fihe mâ fih*, ed. B. Foruzânfar (Tehran: Amir Kabir, 1983), 112, as translated by A.J. Arberry in *Discourses of Rumi* (New York: Samuel Weiser, 1972), 123 or by Wheeler Thackston in *Signs of the Unseen: The Discourses of Jalalddin Rumi* (Putney, VT: Threshold Books, 1994), 117. Here, Rumi appears to refer to his composition of poetry, and/or his discussion of theosophical points; he needs a customer who will fit the text he's weaving.

THE HEART like grain   Ghazal 181

Del cho dâne mâ mesâl-e âsyâ

Ramal mahzuf: | ¯ ˘ ¯ ¯ | ¯ ˘ ¯ ¯ | ¯ ˘ ¯ ||

For the supposed circumstances in which this poem was composed, see Aflâki, *Manâqeb al-'ârefin,* ed. Tahsin Yazıcı, 2 vols. (Ankara, 1959; reprinted Tehran: Donyâ-ye Ketâb, 1983), 370–1. This work can now be consulted in an excellent full English translation: *The Feats of the Knowers of God,* tr. John O'Kane (Leiden: Brill, 2002), 256–7. Because this work was compiled on the basis of testimony of individuals many decades after the fact with little effort to distinguish between what was plausible and what was not, it is not reliable in all details, including the circumstances of composition of individual poems. That said, the composition and/or performance of this poem in *samâ'* at a mill would seem to make sense, as the metaphor of spinning applies nicely to the practice of Mevlevi turning. The English translation here is based on a four-syllable line.

V. POEMS OF LOSS AND CONFUSION

GO LAY YOUR HEAD on your pillow, let me be alone   Ghazal 2039

Row sar beneh be-bâlin tanhâ marâ rahâ kon

Mozâre' akhrab al-sadrayn : | ¯ ¯ ˘ | ¯ ˘ ¯ ¯ | ¯ ¯ ˘ | ¯ ˘ ¯ ¯ ||

Aflâki's explanation of the circumstances of composition of this poem, however improbable, are given in *Manâqeb,* ed. Tahsin Yazıcı (Tehran: Donyâ-ye Ketâb, 1983), 589–90, as translated in *The Feats of the Knowers of God,* tr. John O'Kane (Leiden: Brill, 2002), 402–4. According to Aflâki, it was the last ghazal composed by Rumi, on his death bed, written down by Hosâm al-Din. Sultan Valad, Rumi's son, was obviously distressed at the imminent demise of his father, and would not leave his side. Rumi wished to assure Sultan Valad that he felt well, and that Sultan Valad could go lie down. The content of the poem fits far more closely with the period of Rumi's inconsolable grief after the final disappearance of Shams.

In ancient folklore, an emerald was believed to repulse dragons; its sparkling reflection blinded the dragon, or he would see his own reflection in it and be deceived into thinking that another dragon was staking the territory.

"Bu 'Ali" and "Bu 'Alâ" may allude to the famous wise philosopher, Avicenna (Abu 'Ali ibn Sinâ), and the rationalist, materialist poet, Abu 'Alâ al-Ma'arri, respectively. Alternatively, we might translate them as "such a one" and "so and so."

IT'S STRANGE! Where'd that gorgeous heartbreaker go   Ghazal 677
'Ajab ân delbar-e zibâ kojâ shod
Hazaj mahzuf: | ˇ - - - | ˇ - - - | ˇ - - ||

Another poem evidently composed after one of the two times when Shams disappeared from Konya.

The beloved is compared to a tall, supple cypress tree, and the Sufi shaykh to the beloved.

I'M MAD about, just crazy   Ghazal 1493
Mâ 'âsheq o sar gashte vo shaydâ-ye dameshq-im
Hazaj akhrab makfuf mahzuf: | - - ˇ ˇ | - - ˇ ˇ | - - ˇ ˇ | - - ||

It would appear that some earlier Arabic poems in praise of Damascus inspired Rumi in this ghazal, though he himself had also spent time studying in the city. Aflâki reports (*Manâqeb*, 698–9) in *The Feats of the Knowers of God*, tr. John O'Kane (Leiden: Brill, 2002), 484–5, that this poem was composed on the road to Syria as Rumi went in search of Shams. Many of the locations mentioned, such as the names of the various city gates, are well-known sites in and around the city; a description of them is given in Lewis, *Rumi: Past and Present, East and West* (Oxford: Oneworld, 2000), 195, to which may be added the following.

"Uthman's Codex" (*moshaf 'Osmân*): 'Uthmān, the third caliph of Islam and head of the community from 644 to 655, standardized the text of the Koran, creating an official version that harmonized the variant readings of the professional Koran reciters. A handful of copies of this codex were promulgated to various important Muslim cities, including Damascus. A copy of the codex purporting to be the one that Uthman sent, was kept in the Umayyad Mosque in Damascus, and historians or travelers report having seen the manuscript (Ibn Battūta), though Ibn Kathīr says in his *Faḍā'il al-Qur'ān* that the manuscript was brought to Damascus from Tiberias in 518 A.H./1124 C.E., indicating that the original copy in Damascus must have been moved or destroyed. The poem of Rumi confirms that there was such a manuscript in his day known as Uthman's Codex.

Mizza was a mountain outside Damascus, now a neighborhood incorporated in the modern city.

"Master of Damascus" (*Mowlâ-ye Dameshq*): Apparently an allusion to Rumi's own title among his disciples, as Master of Rum (*Mowlâ-ye Rum*). Instead, he would rather be master of Damascus, if that is where he can be disciple to Shams.

NIGHT AND day   Ghazal 302
Dar havâ-yat bi-qarâr-am ruz o shab
Ramal mahzuf: | ‾ ˇ ‾ ‾ | ‾ ˇ ‾ ‾ | ‾ ˇ ‾ ||

"To drive the night and day to love distraction": That is, to make them like Majnun, the "possessed", who is proverbial for lovesickness in Islamicate cultures. The famous lover of Layli, he pines away for her in the desert, living like a hermit among the animals and singing poems of love night and day.

I MANAGE FINE with no others around   Ghazal 553
Bi-hamegân be-sar shavad bi to be sar nemi-shavad
Rajaz: | ‾ ˇ ˇ ‾ | ˇ ‾ ˇ ‾ | ‾ ˇ ˇ ‾ | ˇ ‾ ˇ ‾ ||

VI. POEMS FROM DISCIPLE TO MASTER

I HAVE THIS friend   Ghazal 37
Yâr marâ ghâr marâ 'eshq-e jegar-kh^w âr marâ
Sari' matvi: | ‾ ˇ ˇ ‾ | ‾ ˇ ˇ ‾ | ‾ ˇ ˇ ‾ | ‾ ˇ ˇ ‾ ||

The two friends in the cave is an allusion to an episode mentioned in Koran 9:40, describing Muhammad's flight from Mecca with Abu Bakr. As the pagan Meccans pursued Muhammad, attempting to kill him, they hid in a cave. A spider is said to have spun a web over the entrance, making it appear as though no one had entered the cave for some time, so the pursuers did not look inside.

"The breast laid open": from Koran 94:1 refers in the first instance to revelation sent down by God when Muhammad was in trying circumstances, which caused his breast to dilate with joy. The biographical tradition also preserves a story about an angel opening up the chest of Muhammad to remove his heart, wash it to purify it from sin, and replace it.

From the last line, we may conclude that this poem was intended to accompany a session of turning (*samâ'*). It apparently dates to one of the two times Shams disappeared from Konya.

O JOSEPH (sweet the name!)   Ghazal 4
Ay Yusof-e khʷosh nâm-e mâ khʷosh mi-ravi bar bâm-e mâ
Rajaz: | ` - - ˘ - ` | ` - - ˘ - ` | ` - - ˘ - ` | ` - - ˘ - ` ||

The "Joseph" in this poem, as everywhere else Rumi invokes this name, is the Koranic Joseph, whose story is told in Sura 12 of the Koran (and also, of course, in the Bible). He is an emblem of beauty and chaste purity (for rejecting the advances of Potiphar's wife). He is also divinely guided, seeing dreams of his own greatness and interpreting dreams for the Pharoah. The spiritual guide or mystic beloved is often compared to Joseph. He was cast by his brothers into a well because he had received a colored cloak from his father, Jacob, as an indication that Joseph was his father's pride and joy. The scent of Joseph's shirt/coat and Joseph in the well are common motifs in Persian poetry.

ICON, I CAN NEVER get my fill of you   Ghazal 1046
Na-gashtam az to hargez ay sanam sir
Hazaj mahzuf: | ˘ - - - | ˘ - - - | ˘ - - ||

Isrâfil is an archangel mentioned in the Hadith, responsible for blowing the trumpet that announces the Day of Resurrection from a holy spot in Jerusalem. This trumpet blast of Resurrection is mentioned in the Koran (36:49–53 and 69:13–19). Etymologically, the name perhaps derives from Hebrew "seraph," but Israfil has also been associated with the archangel Raphael in Judeo-Christian tradition.

"Jamshid's grail" (*jâm-e jam*): The mythical Persian king, Jamshid, possessed a goblet or grail in which he could see all the events of the world (it is now the name of the international television channel of the Islamic Republic of Iran). For the legend of the Persian king Jamshid, see Ferdowsi, *Shahnameh: The Persian Book of Kings*, trans. Dick Davis (New York: Viking, 2006).

I PAINT ICONS   Ghazal 1462
Suratgar-e naqqâsh-am har lahze boti mi-sâzam
Hazaj akhrab al-sadrayn: | ‾ ˘ ˘ | ˘ ‾ ‾ ‾ | ‾ ˘ ˘ | ˘ ‾ ‾ ‾ ||

I sleep and wake in love's afflictions   Ghazal 319
Umsī wa a'bi'u bi-l-jawá ata'aḏḥḏḥabu
Rajaz: | ˘ ˘ ‾ ˘ ‾ | ˘ ˘ ‾ ˘ ‾ | ˘ ‾ ˘ ˘ ‾ || (in Arabic)

MY LIFEBLOOD, my world   Ghazal 3165
Jân o jahân dush kojâ bude'i
Sari': | ‾ ˘ ˘ ‾ | ‾ ˘ ˘ ‾ | ‾ ˘ ˘ ||

LOVER, COME here. Today you are ours   Ghazal 2716
Biâ jânâ ke emruz ân-e mâ'i
Hazaj mahzuf: | ˘ ‾ ‾ ‾ | ˘ ‾ ‾ ‾ | ˘ ‾ ‾ ||

The ghazal formula requires that the first and second hemistich of the opening line rhyme with one another, and this rhyme must be retained in the second hemistich of every line throughout the poem. In this particular poem, the second hemistich of each line consists of a repeated phrase ("X thou art, X thou art, X"), where each and every two-syllable X throughout the poem rhymes with all the others, constituting a kind of litany of hyper-rhymes. In addition, the first hemistich of lines 3 through 5 also share an ending with each other ("for him/it" = *u râ*), which is not required by the ghazal form, and hence represents an additional rhetorical device in this poem. Line 6 replaces the "him" with "God" (*khodâ râ*) at the end of the first hemistich, thus creating an intense series of parallelisms and sonorities. The last line, rather than saying "God thou art," replaces "thou" with the imperative: "Act like God/a Lord."

"The Bird of Royal Omen/Royal Bird (*Homâ*)": A mythical bird whose shadow blesses all who are touched by it, and which signifies the divine right of the king.

VII. POEMS FROM MASTER TO DISCIPLE

Chelebi is a Turkish title, akin to "master," and here signifies Hosâm al-Din Chelebi, the companion to whom Rumi dictated the *Masnavi,* and to whom he delegated a leading role in the community of disciples. "Chelebi" was also later used as a title for the male descendants of Sultan Valad, Rumi's son. The position of Grand Chelebi, chosen from Rumi's lineage, was the title given to the head of the Mevlevi Order. These lines seem to be from an initiation poem.

"Poverty" refers to the voluntary poverty that allows the adept to practice detachment from worldly goods.

DO YOU, novice, wish to turn dung to musk?

From Masnavi Book 5: 2472–9

Khotan is a region, or kingdom, in China along the silk route. It is an oasis, noted for mulberries and evidently for its good pastures. It is known for its musk deer, and hence musk is associated in particular with China and Khotan.

TAKE LOVE'S chalice and on you go   Ghazal 2179
To jâm-e 'eshq râ be-stân o mi-row
Hazaj: | ˇ – – – | ˇ – – – | ˇ – – ||

DIDN'T I TELL you   Ghazal 1725
Na-goftam-at ma-row ânjâ ke âshnâ-t man-am
Mojtass: | ˇ – ˇ – | ˇ ˇ – – | ˇ – ˇ ˇ – | ˇ ˇ – ||

The very unlikely report attributed to Hosâm al-Din Chelebi by Aflâki in *Manâqeb*, ed. Yazıcı›, 147–9, and given in translation by John O'Kane in *The Feats of the Knowers of God* (Leiden: Brill, 2002), 103–4, indicates that this poem was composed for the Seljuq Sultan Rokn al-Din, as he was strangled by the "Tatar" Mongols.

AND WHO He asked is at the door?   Ghazal 436
Goftâ ke kist bar dar goftam kamin gholâm-at
Mozâre' akhrab al-sadrayn: | – – ˇ | – ˇ – – | – – ˇ | – ˇ – – ||

This poem is as much a conversation of the disciple with the master as it is the inverse, especially insofar as the poem is related in the first person through the persona of the disciple. However, it begins with the question of the master, and relates a symbolic encounter in which the speaker of the poem must silence himself for fear of revealing too much of the overpowering mystical truth he has experienced.

"The fragrance in your chalice": Foruzanfar's edition reads *jân-at* ("your soul"), which slightly violates the rhyme of the poem. A.J. Arberry therefore amended this to read *jâm-at* ("your chalice") in his translation, as given in *Mystical Poems of Rūmī*, v. 1 (Chicago: University of Chicago Press, 1968), 178. This response poem evokes a petitioner seeking entrance to the court, and since the royal court is the site of wine and banquets and jewel-encrusted goblets, the reading "your chalice" (*jâm-at*) may be correct. On the other hand, "the fragrance of your spirit" is also an attractive reading, and is not improbable, given the poetic license Rumi sometimes takes.

HERE A FEW, there a few   Ghazal 819
Andak andak jam'-e mastân mi-resand
Ramal: | ‾ ˘ ‾ ‾ | ‾ ˘ ‾ ‾ | ‾ ˘ ‾ ||

The poem suggests an initiation ritual of sorts, perhaps fasting or serving in the kitchen (initiates to the Mevlevi order, at least in later years, would serve in the Mevlevi kitchen for one thousand days before being allowed to "whirl" in turning ceremonies). Initiates would be male, typically adolscents, and they are therefore imagined in this poem like the Hellenistic ephebe. In Persian ghazal poetry, the beloved is often a beautiful adolescent boy, and poets would often play with this convention.

CARAVANEER! See the camels all on down the line, a whole train, drunk
                                                            Ghazal 390
Sârebânâ oshtorân bin sar-be-sar qatâr-e mast
Ramal: | ‾ ˘ ‾ ‾ | ‾ ˘ ‾ ‾ | ‾ ˘ ‾ ‾ | ‾ ˘ ‾ ||

WHOEVER LEAVES our circle for another place   Ghazal 794
Har ke az halqe-ye mâ jâ-ye degar bogrizad
Ramal makhbun: | ‾ ˘ ‾ ‾ | ˘ ˘ ‾ ‾ | ˘ ˘ ‾ ‾ | ˘ ˘ ‾ ||

"Fear of the reaper": The archangel 'Azrâ'il is the angel of death in Persian tradition. It is related in the traditions of the Prophet (Hadith) that when

God wants to seize a servant's life from a certain place on earth, he makes it necessary for that servant to travel there. There is a story about this in Rumi's *Masnavi,* Book 1: 956–70.

YOU WHO SUPPOSED steam   Ghazal 2382

Ay bokhâri râ to jân pendâshte

Ramal: | ‾ ˇ ‾ ‾ | ‾ ˇ ‾ ‾ | ‾ ˇ ‾ ||

The family of Rumi were preachers, and Rumi was well practiced in this art. Some of the sermons he gave for his disciples are recorded in his *Majâles-e sab'e* (an example of one of them is translated in Lewis, *Rumi: Past and Present,* 130–33). A preacher might rely upon the expectations of the homiletic genre to lull his audience into a misperception about what was being said, as in this poem.

Korah (Qārūn) appears in the Koran (28:76–82) as a fabulously wealthy man who grew proud, thinking that his treasures were a reward for his knowledge. Though warned by his people to act humbly and charitably, and that worldly possessions would not profit him in the next world, he persisted in his arrogance and in his rebellion against Moses and Aaron, and was eventually swallowed up by the earth.

VIII. POEMS FROM MASTER TO MASTER

Rumi speaks of Shams al-Din Tabrizi as a great spiritual teacher and master, and even composes many of his poems in the voice of Shams al-Din. But Rumi also spoke of two other men as sources of spiritual inspiration or guides, first Salâh al-Din Zarkub and then Hosâm al-Din Chelebi. The way that Rumi spoke of these latter two individuals has been puzzling to some of his disciples, as well as scholars, insofar as the intellectual and spiritual achievements of Rumi seem to dwarf theirs. At times, Rumi adopts the voice of wisdom and insight, not in a didactic tone as one might address disciples, but rather as if addressing others of similar insight. Indeed, Shams often describes the relationship between himself and Rumi as one of relative equals in his *Maqâlât.* See William Chittick's translation, *Me and Rumi: The Autobiography of Shams-i Tabrizi* (Louisville, KY: Fons Vitae, 2004), and also Lewis, *Rumi: Past and Present* (Oxford: Oneworld, 2000), 162–71.

I WAS DEAD, came back to life   Ghazal 1393
Morde bodam zende shodam gerye bodam khande shodam
Sari' matvi: | - ˇ ˇ - | - ˇ ˇ - | - ˇ ˇ - | - ˇ ˇ - ||

"Joseph": See the note under Poems from Disciple to Master, *Ay Yusof-e kh^w osh
nâm-e mâ kh^w osh mi-ravi bar bâm-e mâ*, Ghazal 4 [O Joseph (sweet the name!)].

YOU THERE, checkmated by the king of love   Ghazal 378
Ay gashte ze shâh-e 'eshq shahmât
Hazaj akhrab maqbuz mahzuf: | ˇ - - - | - ˇ - ˇ | - - ||

YOU, LEADER of the prayers to Love   Ghazal 2933
Ay ânk emâm-e 'eshqi takbir kon ke masti
Mozâre' akhrab al-sadrayn: | - - ˇ | - ˇ - - | - - ˇ | - ˇ - - ||

The Imam leads the prayer, usually announced by the muezzin from the
minaret with the chant, "God is Great" (*Allâhu akbar*). The poem, however,
represents a call for the prayer of love, a mystical rather than ritual approach
to communion.

"Howlessness" (*bi-chegune*) evokes an epithet for God, who should not be
asked to explain his doings – it would be impudent and impertinent for con-
tingent creatures to demand this information, which, in any case, is beyond
their comprehension.

THAT REDCLOAK   Ghazal 650
Ân sorkh qabâ'i ke cho mah pâr bar âmad
Hazaj akhrab makfuf mahzuf: | - - ˇ ˇ | - - ˇ ˇ | - - ˇ ˇ | - - ||

The later Mevlevis wore a particular color of ceremonial cloak for their turning
ceremony, but this poem apparently alludes to Salâh al-Din Zarkub, who became
the focus of Rumi's devotions after the disappearance of Shams al-Din Tabrizi.

"Abyssinian age" (*dowrân-e habash*) and "fair Greek" (*rumi*): The dark
complexion of the Abyssinians (Ethiopians) and the light complexion of the
Greeks (the inhabitants of Anatolia) is a metaphor for night and day here.
This occurs elsewhere in Rumi's poetry, sometimes with East Africans
(*zangi*) or Abyssinians representing dark skin. In addition, the Abyssinians

and Greeks both represent non-Muslim populations. Among other ethnic groups sometimes evoked for various qualities, not only skin color, we also find Arab, Turk, Armenian, Persian, Kurd and Indian. The word *rumi* also sometimes indicates geographic region, Anatolian, rather than an ethnicity, in contrast to Syrian, or in one poem to city toponymics (Marghzi, Râzi).

In the end time   Ghazal 1210
Nist dar âkhar-zamân faryâd-ras
Ramal mahzuf: | ‾ ˇ ‾ ‾ | ‾ ˇ ‾ ‾ | ‾ ˇ ‾ ||

The hagiographer Aflâki gives the circumstances of composition of this poem, explaining that Rumi was whirling in *samâ'*. See *Manâqeb al-'ârefin*, ed. Tahsin Yazıcı (Tehran: Donyâ-ye Ketâb, 1983), 736 and the English version translated by John O'Kane as *The Feats of the Knowers of God* (Leiden: Brill, 2002), 513. The poem would appear to date from some time after the final disappearance of Shams from Konya (i.e. from about 1248), until the death of Salâh al-Din in 1258.

Bereft of you both earth and sky shed tears!   Ghazal 2364
Ay ze hejrân-at zamin o âsemân be-griste
Ramal mahzuf: | ‾ ˇ ‾ ‾ | ‾ ˇ ‾ ‾ | ‾ ˇ ‾ ‾ | ‾ ˇ ‾ ||

This poem was said to have been recited at the funeral of Salâh al-Din; see *The Feats of the Knowers of God*, tr. John O'Kane (Leiden: Brill, 2002), 508–10.

O LIGHT OF Truth, Hosâm al-Din! Let's add

From *Masnavi* Book 1: 2934–8

Hosâm al-Din was the spiritual companion of Rumi after the disappearance of Shams and the death of Salâh al-Din Zarkub. It was at the request of Hosâm al-Din, whom Rumi titled "Light of the Faith," that the *Masnavi* was composed.

"Pir": an adjective meaning "old" as applied to a person, but also a noun meaning "elder", and, in the Sufi context, a spiritual guide. It is the equivalent of the Arabic term *shaykh*.

SO, IN EVERY AGE, a saint arises   From *Masnavi* Book 2: 819–24

Rumi taught that there was a hierarchy of saints, with the spiritual axis, or "pole" (*qotb*), of the age being the pivot around whom the spiritual life of the universe turned. He was often hidden, unknown or unrecognized by people, though the life of the spirit depended upon him. This doctrine of the pole, or perfect man, found some favor among many Sufis, but was not necessarily approved by the orthodoxy.

The terminology used in this poem includes:

Valī = saint (friend of God), guardian.

Imām = for Shiites, a descendant of Muhammad and divinely inspired ruler of the community, the rightful authority rather than the caliph. For Sunnis, it is simply a prayer leader, behind whom the congregation performs the ritual prayers.

'Umar = the second caliph, or successor to Muhammad as head of the community of Islam. Because the Shiites believed 'Ali should rightfully have been appointed, 'Umar is considered a caliph by Sunnis but not by Shiites.

'Alī = the son-in-law and cousin of the Prophet, as well as the third man elected caliph after the death of the Prophet. He is accepted by both Sunnis and Shiites, but is held by Shiites to have been appointed by Muhammad as his successor, and invested with mystical authority, because he received oral teachings from the Prophet which were not necessarily included in the Koran.

Mahdī = the "rightly guided one," a figure of both Sunni and Shiite eschatology, who will help usher in justice in the days of the end.

IX. POEMS OF DREAMS AND VISIONS

Mansur on this title page refers to Hallâj, executed in Baghdad in 922 for the blasphemy of speaking openly about his mystical identification with God. Pharoah, meanwhile, though he was lord of his kingdom, spoke real blasphemy because of his haughtiness and opposition to Moses.

The unbelievers tried to burn Abraham in the fire, but he found it to be cool, because of God's protection (Koran 21:67–9). For Rumi's treatment of Abraham, see John Renard, *All the King's Falcons: Rumi on Prophets and Revelation* (Albany: State University of New York Press, 1994), 47–58.

HOW COULD I know this melancholy   Ghazal 1855
Che dânestam ke in sowdâ marâ z-in sân konad majnun
Hazaj: | ˘ - - - | ˘ - - - | ˘ - - - | ˘ - - - ||

Korah (Qārūn), in the Koran, is a wealthy man swallowed up by the earth for his pride (see the description above under Poems from Master to Disciple, *Ay bokhâri râ to jân pendâshte* Ghazal 2382). In addition to the Koranic version of the story, it also occurs in briefer form in the Bible (Numbers 26:9–11), where Korah leads a rebellion against Moses and Aaron and is swallowed up by the earth for it. There may also be some echo of the Greek legend of Croesus, king of Lydia, in the name Korah.

The staving in of the ship's plank alludes to the Koranic story of Moses and Khizr (18:65–82), which in turn was used as a metaphor of the relationship of Rumi and Shams (see Lewis, *Rumi: Past and Present*, 33–5).

"Howlessness" (*bi-chun*): An epithet for God. See Poems from Master to Master, *Ay ânk emâm-e 'eshqi takbir kon ke masti*, Ghazal 2933.

It has been ventured that opium (*afyun*) was used as an antidote to drowning, or to madness. Perhaps here the vision described is compared to a hallucinogenic experience. In any case, "a froth" (*kaff-i*) can here mean both the foam of the sea and also a handful, or palmful.

TODAY I SAW him   Ghazal 19
Emruz didam yâr râ ân rownaq-e har kâr râ
Rajaz: | ‾ ˘ ˘ | ‾ ˘ ˘ | ‾ ˘ ˘ | ‾ ˘ ˘ ||

Mustafâ, "the chosen one," is an epithet of the Prophet, Muhammad. The ladder to clamber onto the heavens would enable the speaker of the poem to follow the Prophet on his *mi'râj*, or miraculous journey into the heavens, where he came into the near presence of the divine essence (as described in Koran 53:5–18).

O FRIEND, within whom I have disappeared!   Ghazal 1507
Ayâ yâri ke dar to nâ-padid-am
Hazaj mahzuf: | ˘ ‾ ‾ ‾ | ˘ ‾ ‾ ‾ | ˘ ‾ ‾ ||

The story of Potiphar's wife, as related in the Koran, includes a scene in which the wife, after her husband has determined her at fault in trying to seduce Joseph, invites her ladyfriends for a banquet, so that they can see Joseph's beauty for themselves and stop blaming her for her behavior. They are cutting citrons to eat when Joseph is called in. Astonished at his beauty, they cut their own hands instead of the citrus fruit they are holding (see Koran 12:30–2). Three famous Sufi masters of the ninth and tenth centuries C.E. are evoked at the end of the poem: the ascetic mystical teacher Dhū al-Nūn of Egypt (d. 861); Junayd (d. 910), the expounder of the "sober" school of Sufism (in contrast to the "drunken" ecstaticism of Hallāj); and Bāyazid (Abū Yazīd) Bastāmī (d. c. 874), a visionary mystic who is associated with the doctrine of effacement *(fanā)* and with ecstatic sayings, such as "Glory be to me" *(subhānī)*.

HERE'S JOSEPH'S coat   Ghazal 997
Pirhan-e Yusof o bu mi-resad
Sari' matvi maksuf: | ‾ ˇ ˇ ˇ | ‾ ˇ ˇ ˇ | ‾ ˇ ˇ ||

The story of Joseph is given in the Koran, Sura 12, but see the note on Joseph under Poems from Disciple to Master, *Ay Yusof-e khʷosh nâm-e mâ khʷosh miravi bar bâm-e mâ*, Ghazal 4.

Hallâj was a Persian Sufi put to death in Baghdad in 922 C.E. for his ecstatic revelation of mystic insight, which appeared blasphemous to orthodox theology. It included the famous phrase "I am Truth/God" *(anā al-haqq)*.

WE ARE LOVE'S FLAME that has reached the wax   Ghazal 1481
Mâ âtash-e 'eshq-im ke dar mum residim
Hazaj akhrab makfuf: | ‾ ‾ ˇ ˇ | ‾ ‾ ˇ ˇ | ‾ ‾ ˇ ˇ | ‾ ‾ ||

"The Throne Verse" is a name given to verse 255 of Surat al-Baqara in the Koran (2:255). It emphasizes the sanctification of God above his creatures and the creation, and his all-encompassing knowledge of them and their affairs, which he watches over from his throne, which extends over heaven and earth. The verse is much quoted in devotional contexts, as a reminder that humans only have access to that portion of the divine knowledge which God wills to bestow upon them. "The Living One" *(al-hayy)* and "the Self-Subsisting" *(al-qayyūm)* are epithets of God in this verse.

Zonnâr is a belt or cord associated with Zoroastrians or Christians and their religious rites, but especially with wine-drinking. It is therefore a symbol of paganism, or of the mystic ministrations of the Sufi Shaykh.

"Qaysar-e Rumi" ("the Anatolian Caesar") may signify the Emperor of Byzantium, or Christendom, whose symbolic and ritual Christian garb is stripped off by the poet. It may also allude to the ruler of Seljuq Anatolia, since the Seljuq Sultan 'Alâ al-Din Kay Qobâd had in 1224–6 built a palace called Qobâdiyye in the city of Kayseri (Qaysari).

I'M OUT OF my senses and you are smashed   Ghazal 2309
Man bi-kh^wod o to bi-kh^wod mârâ ki barad khâne
Hazaj akhrab sâlem: | ‾‾˘ | ˘‾‾‾ | ‾‾˘ | ˘‾‾‾ ||

"The Moaning Pillar" (*oston-e hannâne*): A tradition relates that the Prophet Muhammad would lean on a certain tree trunk in the Prophet's Mosque in Medina while he preached. When a pulpit was later constructed, this tree trunk was heard to moan in its separation from the touch of the Prophet.

I HAVE SEEN a vision, worthy of attention and praise!   Ghazal 1839
Vâqe'e'i be-dide-am lâyeq-e lotf o âfarin
Rajaz matvi makhbun: | ‾˘˘‾ | ˘‾˘‾ | ‾˘˘‾ | ˘‾˘‾ ||

The term *vâqe'e* suggests a kind of dream or vision that reveals or predicts a true event. Dream interpretation was often practiced as a profession by individuals thought to have a talent or susceptibility for it (*mo'abber*), here rendered as "mantic." Based upon the address at the end of the poem, this would appear to refer to Hosâm al-Din Chelebi, to whom the *Masnavi* was dictated by Rumi.

The Koranic verses cited in the poem (80:39 and 88:9) describe the countenances of the faithful believers, on the judgment day and in paradise, respectively.

The date 5 Dhū al-Qaʿda 654 A.H. corresponds to 24 November 1256 C.E. In June of that year (Jumādī al-thānī), basaltic magma erupted from the ground in the Harrat Rahat area between Mecca and Medina, causing increasingly strong and frequent tremors for four days, until finally a large earthquake shook Medina on 5 Jumadi al-thani as people gathered for the Friday prayers. For two months after that, volcanic eruptions spewed lava that came within eight kilometers of Medina itself. It spread as a red-blue river of two meters' depth, which brightly lit up the night sky for miles around, making it appear as if the sun shone on the Kaaba at nighttime. Just a few months later, in an unrelated event, on 1 Ramadan (22 September), in an unrelated event, the Prophet's Mosque was destroyed by fire. In the same year the Tigris flooded Baghdad, the city of the Abbasid caliphate, which the Mongols would soon conquer in February 1258. Rebuilding of the Prophet's Mosque in Medina was delayed due to the Mongol invasions.

"Tatars" evidently refers to the Mongol troops; Armenians in Cilicia continued to be hostile to the Seljuq rulers. On Seljuq Anatolia in the time of Rumi, see Lewis, *Rumi: Past and Present*, 78–81, 279–82, etc.

THIS WORLD would be engulfed in flames, if the lover's soul would speak
Ghazal 527

Gar jân-e 'âsheq dam zanad âtash dar in 'âlam zanad
Rajaz: | - - ˇ - | - - ˇ - | - - ˇ - | - - ˇ - ||

This poem is modeled on one by Sanâ'i, whom Rumi often speaks of highly as a poetic precursor and mystical thinker. It is an eschatological vision of the passing away of the world and the creation of a new one at the Resurrection.

"East of it": In the Koran (19:26) Mary withdrew from her people to the east and covered herself with a veil, at which point a spirit of the Lord appeared to the Virgin in human form, with the announcement that she was destined to bear a sanctified son.

"Scion of the unseen": *pure-ye adham* (Scion of Adham = blackness), would appear to be a reference to Ibrahīm ibn Adham (Abraham son of Adham), a ninth-century ascetic Sufi from Balkh, who, according to legend (echoing the legend of the Buddha), was a prince who gave up his dominion to practice spirituality and voluntary poverty. Called "the Scion of Adham" (*pur-e adham*), Ibrahīm ibn Adham appears in the *Masnavi* as "the Sultan of the Sultans of justice" (*Masnavi* Book 2: 932), and also elsewhere in the ghazals as "Son of Adham" (*pesar-e adham*, e.g. Ghazal 640). The phrase *pure-ye adham* occurs one other time in the ghazals of Rumi (Ghazal 1135), but there is also a similar phrase, *pur-e âdam* (Son of Adam) (Ghazal 859), or the metrically identical phrase *pure-ye âdam* (Ghazal 1615). This reading (Son of Adam = Son of Man) may actually make better sense here, if we allow ourselves to assume a copyist's error in the manuscript.

In Islamic eschatology, Jesus is expected to return in the time of the end to do battle with the anti-Christ (Dajjāl), after which, with the Mahdī, a reign of peace will be ushered in. Rumi speaks of each individual soul having an interior Jesus waiting to be born (*Fihe mâ fih*, ed. Foruzânfar, 21 and also *Masnavi* Book 2: 450), but the Messiah carried by Mary also has a role in the Resurrection. This Messiah is not of water and clay, but is beyond space. The entire world is pregnant with the soul of soul carried by Mary, and the world will give birth to another world at the time of the Resurrection (*Masnavi* Book 2: 1183–8). Elsewhere in the *Masnavi* (3: 3771–82), the Holy Spirit tells Mary, who runs from the human shape it has assumed to impregnate her, "Do not flee from my being into the Void [pre-existent nothingness = *'adam*]. In the Void, I am the king and standard-bearer. My home and foundation and home is in nothingness; it's only a form of mine that stands before your ladyship. Mary! Look on my difficult form: I am the crescent moon as well as an imagination in your heart. When this image enters your heart and inhabits it, it remains with you, no matter what direction you flee. Except for a superficial and vain imagination, which is like unto a false and fleeting dawn. However, I am the true and radiant dawn from the light of the Lord, whom no night can touch with darkness ... You take refuge in God from me, but I am the epitome of refuge in pre-eternity ... you suppose the Friend to be a stranger and joy to be called a sorrow."

X. POEMS ON THE RELIGION OF LOVE: WAYS OF REASON, MODES OF LOVE

In the poem excerpts on the title page of this chapter, Vaxsh is mentioned. This is the birthplace of Rumi, on the Vaxshab river, in what is now Tajikistan. He left the area when he was a boy, eventually settling in Anatolia, never to return home. The legend that he was born in Balkh is contradicted by what Bahâ al-Din Valad, Rumi's father, wrote.

Also mentioned here is Fakhr al-Din Râzi, the theologian, who died in 1209, after writing a penitent will and testament. He had been considered arrogant, in part for over-reliance on his own reason.

Abū Hanīfa and Shāfi'ī were founders of two of the canonical Sunni schools of law. Hence they represent the application of reason and systematization to the study of religious knowledge, that produced rules of behavior, creeds and theology. Specifically, Rumi followed the Hanafī school and Shams followed the Shāfi'ī school.

LOVE RESIDES not in learning Ghazal 395
'Eshq andar fazl o 'elm o daftar o owrâq nist
Ramal mahzuf: | ⁻ ˇ ⁻ ⁻ | ⁻ ˇ ⁻ ⁻ | ⁻ ˇ ⁻ ⁻ | ⁻ ˇ ⁻ ||

THE SEEKER of the Court of God's like this
From *Masnavi* Book 3: 4658–63

YOU ATTAIN to knowledge by argument From *Masnavi* Book 5: 1062–7

Sohbat is the Sufi concept of companionship with the *pir*, or elder – the spiritual guide. By being with the guide, hearing what he says and watching what he does and how he reacts to things, the disciple gradually may learn the spirituality that the guide has learned.

THE EYE wants something new to see Ghazal 617
Cheshm az pay-e ân bâyad tâ chiz-e 'ajab binad
Hazaj akhrab al-sadrayn: | ⁻ ⁻ ˇ | ˇ ⁻ ⁻ ⁻ | ⁻ ⁻ ˇ | ˇ ⁻ ⁻ ⁻ ||

"The Black Stone" (here *sang-e siah*, though properly *al-hajar al-aswad*) of the Kaaba is a corner stone of that building, to kiss which is the desire of pilgrims circumambulating the Kaaba.

THE THINKER is always at pains to make his mark Ghazal 1957
Hast 'âqel har zamâni dar gham-e paydâ shodan
Ramal mahzuf: | ⁻ ˇ ⁻ ⁻ | ⁻ ˇ ⁻ ⁻ | ⁻ ˇ ⁻ ⁻ | ⁻ ˇ ⁻ ||

LET GO ALL your scheming, lover Ghazal 2131
Hilat rahâ kon 'âsheqâ divâne show divâne show
Rajaz: | ⁻ ⁻ ˇ ⁻ | ⁻ ⁻ ˇ ⁻ | ⁻ ⁻ ˇ ⁻ | ⁻ ⁻ ˇ ⁻ ||

The "Night of the Grave" (*laylat al-qabr*): On the first night of burial, the angels of the grave, Nakir and Munkar, visit the deceased soul in the grave. The soul will not be dispatched to heaven or hell until the final judgement of the Resurrection, but must reply correctly to questions asked about religion and the nature of Muhammad on that first night of the grave, or face torment. This is not a doctrine of the Koran, but was elaborated later.

"The Night of Power" (*Lailat al-qadr*): Traditionally believed to be the night when revelation came to the Prophet, in the last part of Ramadan. The Koran (see 97:1–5) says that God's angels and spirit descend to bless every endeavor on this night.

"The Chosen One" (Mustafâ) is an epithet of Muhammad, the Prophet.

"The Moaning Pillar": According to tradition, Muhammad would lean on a tree trunk in the mosque at Medina as he preached. When a pulpit was constructed, this pillar cried out and is therefore known as the Moaning Pillar (*oston-e hannâne*; literally "the compassionate pillar"), because, even though inanimate, it longed to be in the presence of the Prophet.

Solomon, the heir of David, was granted by the God the ability to understand the language of the birds (Koran 27:16ff).

AMONG LOVERS don't be a wise guy   Ghazal 182
Dar miân-e 'âsheqân 'âqel ma-bâ
Ramal mahzuf: | ⁻ ˇ ⁻ ⁻ | ⁻ ˇ ⁻ ⁻ | ⁻ ˇ ⁻ ||

The Hajj is the pilgrimage to Mecca. Mount Safâ is a small hill in Mecca visited by the pilgrims during the pilgrimage ritual.

The Pleiades is a constellation associated with poetry, in part because it resembles a necklace of pearls, itself a metaphor for the ghazal – pearls of speech pierced and threaded on a string of meter and rhyme.

A MAN IN love, no matter what he says   From *Masnavi* Book 1: 2880–2

THE GNOSTIC arcs constant toward the King's throne
                                 From *Masnavi* Book 5: 2180, 2191–2

The contrast between the gnostic (*'âref*) and the scholar (*'âlem*) and the ascetic (*zâhed*) is frequently portrayed in Sufi literature. In his discourses, Rumi elaborates further, explaining that the scholar ("the knowing one") shares an attribute with God, insofar as he knows things, and in this respect is superior to a gnostic. A gnostic is a person who did not know and then came to know, which is not an attribute of God, who always was all-knowing. But the gnostic comes to know things that knowledge based on reason cannot know, and in this respect is superior. As for the ascetic person, his asceticism is based on religious knowledge; his turning away from the world is based on a knowledge of the world and its nature. Nevertheless, it is said that a scholar is better than a thousand ascetics, and this is also true, if the scholar has attained to the higher knowledge that comes after asceticism. See *Ketâb-e Fihe mâ fih*, ed. B. Foruzânfar (Tehran: Amir Kabir, 1983), 47. Two English translations, exist: by A.J. Arberry, *Discourses of Rumi* (New York: Samuel Weiser, 1972), 58–9, and by Wheeler Thackston, *Signs of the Unseen: The Discourses of Jalaluddin Rumi* (Putney, VT: Threshold Books, 1994), 49.

IF WORDS made you certain that fire exists   From *Masnavi* Book 2: 860–1

XI. POEMS CELEBRATING UNION

The sacrifice and celebration alluded to in the fragment from Ghazal 2114 suggest the Festival of the Sacrifice (*'Id al-adhâ* or *'Id al-qurbān*), which commemorates Abraham's binding of his son. During this festival (as also on other festive occasions), an animal would be slain and the meat shared with the poor.

MAY THE blessings which flow in all weddings   Ghazal 236
Mobâraki ke bovad dar hame 'arusi-hâ
Mojtass: | ˘ - ˘ - | ˘ ˘ - - | ˘ - ˘ - | ˘ ˘ - ||

This poem was said to be recited on the wedding night (*zefâf*) of Fâteme, the daughter of Salâh al-Din, with the son of Rumi, Sultan Valad. See the description in *The Feats of the Knowers of God*, tr. John O'Kane (Leiden: Brill, 2002), 501–2.

YOU'RE A SPRIG of rose!   Ghazal 1003
Shâkh-e goli bâgh ze to sabz o shâd
Sari' matvi maksuf: | - ˘ ˘ - | - ˘ ˘ - | - ˘ ˘ ||

Kay Qobâd is a mythical Iranian king, but also the regnal name of two of the Seljuq Sultans of Rum during the lifetime of Rumi, 'Alâ al-Din Kay Qobâd I (r. 1219–37) and 'Alâ al-Din Kay Qobâd II (r. 1249–57). This poem may perhaps be dated to the reign of the latter.

In the *Masnavi* (Book 3: 3770), Rumi describes "a lick of pure light" (*donbâle-ye nur-e pâk*) rising up to the stars from the lips of the Holy Spirit as he, in human form announces to a frightened Mary that she would give birth. A few lines further on (lines 3773–4), this spirit (identified with Gabriel) says: "Mary! Look on my difficult form: I am the crescent moon as well as an imagination in your heart. When this image enters your heart and inhabits it, it remains with you, no matter what direction you flee."

ONCE MORE we come like dust adance in air   Ghazal 1720
Bâr-e degar zarre-vâr raqs konân âmadim
Monsareh matvi maksuf: | ⁻ ˘ ˘ ⁻ | ⁻ ˘ ⁻ (ˇ) | ⁻ ˘ ˘ ⁻ | ⁻ ˘ ⁻ ||

DO NOT sleep   Ghazal 296
Ma-khosb ay yâr-e mehmândâr emshab
Hazaj mahzuf: | ˘ ⁻ ⁻ ⁻ | ˘ ⁻ ⁻ ⁻ | ˘ ⁻ ⁻ ||

This poem, in a Polish version done by Tadeusz Miciński, titled *Pieśńo nocy*, was set to music by Karol Szymanowksi in his Symphony # 3, Op. 27. Miciński worked from the German version of Joseph von Hammer-Purgstall. For a treatment of the symphonic lyric text (including Persian transliteration, Hammer-Purgstall's German, a French translation of Miciński's Polish and a modern French rendering) see Wojciech Skalmowski, "Un *samâ'* polonais: le 'Chant de la nuit' de Karol Szymanowski" in *"Mais comment peut-on être persan?" Eléments iraniens en Orient & Occident. Liber amicorum Annette Donckier de Donceel*, ed. C. van Ruymbeke (Louvain: Peeters, 2003), 137–51.

"The winged Ja'far" (*Ja'far-e tayyâr*) is an epithet for Ja'far ibn Abī Tālib, the brother of the Prophet's son-in-law, 'Ali. Ja'far was killed in battle with the Byzantine army in 629, but he continued to hold the battle standard of Islam up against his chest with his upper arms even after both his hands had been cut off. According to tradition, the Prophet Muhammad compared his arms to wings with which he would soar in paradise. His epithet *tayyâr* is similar to the name of the star Altair (*al-tā'ir*, or "flying"), the brightest star in the constellation Aquila, the Flying Eagle (*al-nasr al-tā'ir*). The poet therefore recalls Ja'far-e tayyâr as he sees the Flying Eagle).

TOP OF THE MORNING, you're already smashed!   Ghazal 3153
Z-avval-e bâmdâd sar-masti
Khafif: | ˘ ⁻ ˘ ⁻ | ˘ ⁻ ˘ ⁻ | ˘ ⁻ ˘ ||

TOP OF THE MORNING, you're already smashed!   Ghazal 3154
Z-avval-e bâmdâd sar-masti
Khafif: | ˘ ˘ ‒ ‒ | ˘ ‒ ˘ ‒ | ˘ ˘ ‒ ||

These two poems, both starting with the exact same line, and following the same rhyme and meter, illustrate how Persian poets, among them Rumi, might rework their own material in different directions, for different occasions.

Wine is ubiquitously used by Rumi as a metaphor for mystical intoxication. The beginning section of both poems is addressed in the voice of the disciple to the mystic guide. The first poem comes to a close with silence, since the supra-rational experience cannot be adequately expressed. Rumi frequently ends his poems this way, with a call to himself for silence (for more on the poetics of silence in Rumi, see Fatemeh Keshavarz, *Reading Mystical Lyric* [Columbia: University of South Carolina Press, 1998]). In the second version, the speaking persona of the poem calls upon the Sâqi, or cupbearer, to pour out further wine and carry away conscious reason, so that the sense of mystical intuition will alone remain.

A LITTLE apple   Ghazal 968
Sibaki nim sorkh o nimi zard
Khafif: | ‒ ˘ ‒ ‒ | ˘ ‒ ˘ ‒ | ˘ ˘ ‒ ||

The lover in Persian ghazal poetry is expected to suffer in love, to weep, to waste away as he pines and to have a sallow complexion. The beloved is imperious and cruel, able to do without the lover. Therefore his or her cheeks are red and healthy. Of course, the lover–beloved relationship is a metaphor for the worshipper and God, or, in a more immediate sense, the disciple and the guide.

Three lines in the middle of the poem ("I'm like the thorn ..." *measure the chainmail well!* ") are in Arabic, though there are no lines in Arabic in the next poem in Rumi's *Divân*, which happens to begin with the same opening half-line, and maintains the same rhyme.

EXQUISITE LOVE, what exquisite love we have   Ghazal 95
Zahi 'eshq zahi 'eshq ke mârâ-st khodâ-yâ
Hazaj makfuf mahzuf: | ˘ ‒ ‒ ˘ | ˘ ‒ ‒ ˘ | ˘ ‒ ‒ ˘ | ˘ ‒ ‒ ||

IN THIS COLD and rain   Ghazal 1047
Dar in sarmâ vo bârân yâr khᵂosh-tar
Hazaj mahzuf: | ˘ ⁻ ⁻ ⁻ | ˘ ⁻ ⁻ ⁻ | ˘ ⁻ ⁻ ||

BLISS   Ghazal 2214
Khonak ân dam ke neshinim dar ivân man o to
Ramal makhbun: | ˘ ˘ ⁻ ⁻ | ˘ ˘ ⁻ ⁻ | ˘ ˘ ⁻ ⁻ | ˘ ˘ ⁻ ||

"The airs of Iraq and Khorasan" literally reads: "we are both at this moment/
breath in Iraq and Khorasan, you and I" (*ham dar-in dam be 'erâq-im o khorâsân
man o to*). It may allude to musical modes accompanying the poem to the nay,
but they are associated with the respective regions from which Shams (*'erâq-e
'ajam*, "Persian Iraq," or western Iran, could include Tabriz) and Rumi come.

XII. POEMS ON DEATH AND BEYOND

WHERE HAVE you gone   Ghazal 2707
Kojâ'id ay shahidân-e khodâ'i
Hazaj mahzuf: | ˘ ⁻ ⁻ ⁻ | ˘ ⁻ ⁻ ⁻ | ˘ ⁻ ⁻ ||

Karbala is a town southwest of Baghdad, where Husayn ibn 'Ali, the grand-
son of the Prophet, was killed by the Umayyads. He had gone into battle with
the assertion of backing from the populace, in order to assert his claim as the
sole legitimate caliph, which was held to pass to him from his father 'Ali. He
was slain with a small group of family and followers, denied water to quench
his thirst in the hot sun. The shrine built on the spot of his burial is a place of
pilgrimage for Shiites, who see him as the rightful successor to Muhammad
as head of the Muslim community, after 'Ali, his father, and Hasan, his older
brother. Although Rumi was not a Shiite, this poem (along with other poems
and prayers about the occasion) has been used to commemorate the martyr-
dom of Husayn.
      "Tautly bowed arch": The archery bow is commonly compared to the eye-
brows of the beloved, but here to the inverted bowl of the sky.

YOU FLEW OFF in the end   Ghazal 3051
Be-'âqebat be-paridi o dar nehân rafti
Mojtass: | ˘ ⁻ ˘ ⁻ | ˘ ˘ ⁻ ⁻ | ˘ ⁻ ˘ ⁻ | ˘ ˘ ⁻ ||

The falcon is a special image in Rumi for the noble soul obedient to its lord, the king, and by extension John Renard, *All the King's Falcons* (Albany: State University of New York Press, 1994), 14–15, discusses it as a symbol of Rumi's prophetology, in which connection it is opposed to the owls, which haunt the material world.

AND NOW IT'S time Ghazal 464
Nowbat-e vasl o leqâ-st nowbat-e hashr o baqâ-st
Monsareh matvi maksuf: | – ˘ ˘ – | – ˘ – | – ˘ ˘ – | – ˘ – ||

I DIED TO mineral, joined the realm of plants
From *Masnavi* Book 3: 3901–7

XIII. POEMS ON BIRTHING THE SOUL

HEART Ghazal 563
Delâ nazd-e kasi benshin ke u az del khabar dârad
Hazaj: | ˘ – – – | ˘ – – – | ˘ – – – | ˘ – – – ||

HERE I COME again Ghazal 1390
Bâz âmadam bâz âmadam az pish-e ân yâr âmadam
Rajaz: | – – ˘ – | – – ˘ – | – – ˘ – | – – ˘ – ||

The "four mothers" are the four constituent elements of the material universe, according to the philosophy/physics of antiquity: water, earth, fire and air.

The "seven fathers" are the stages or levels into which it was traditionally believed the heavens of the firmament were divided.

BEFORE THE candle Ghazal 2789
Pish-e sham'-e nur-e jân del hast chun parvâne'i
Ramal mahzuf: | – ˘ – – | – ˘ – – | – ˘ – – | – ˘ – ||

OH, HOW colorless Ghazal 1759
Ah che bi-rang o bi-neshân ke man-am
Khafif mahzuf: | – ˘ – – | ˘ – ˘ – | ˘ ˘ – ||

IT'S WAVES OF LOVE that make the heavens turn

From *Masnavi* Book 5: 3854–9

WITH EACH NEW BREATH the sound of love   Ghazal 463

Har nafas âvâz-e 'eshq mi-rasad az chap o râst

Monsareh matvi maksuf: | ⁻ᵛᵛ⁻ | ⁻ᵛᵛ⁻ | ⁻ᵛᵛ⁻ | ᵛᵛ⁻ ||

Aflâki reports that this poem was praised by the famous Sa'di of Shiraz to the ruler of Shiraz, Malek Shams al-Din. See Aflâki, *Manâqeb*, ed. Yazıcı, 266, and, for English, *The Feats of the Knowers of God*, tr. John O'Kane (Leiden: Brill, 2002), 184–5.

INFUSE OUR veins with love's aqua vitae   Ghazal 1821

Âb-e hayât-e 'eshq râ dar rag-e mâ ravâne kon

Rajaz matvi makhbun: | ⁻ᵛᵛ⁻ | ᵛ⁻ᵛ⁻ | ⁻ᵛᵛ⁻ | ᵛ⁻ᵛ⁻ ||

According to the closing verses of Surat al-Qamar, alluded to here, in paradise the righteous will find themselves amidst gardens and streams, at the court/throne of righteousness in the presence of a potent king.

"Magian wine," or Zoroastrian wine, is associated with the pagan wisdom of the ancient Iranian religious tradition and the practices of the Sasanian court. It appears as a symbol both of blasphemy to Muslim orthodoxy, and as the mystic experience that releases the poet from rationality and opens new horizons on the truth. The wine is served and measured out by the Sâqi, or cupbearer.

INDEX OF FIRST LINES

RUMI: PAST AND PRESENT, EAST AND WEST
The Life, Teachings and Poetry of Jalâl al-Din Rumi
FRANKLIN D. LEWIS

ANNIVERSARY EDITION

The first major biography of Rumi in the English language, Franklin Lewis' award-winning work sets a benchmark in Rumi Studies. In this revised, updated edition celebrating the 800th anniversary of Rumi's birth, Lewis offers an unprecedented breadth of coverage, examining Rumi's life and times, his legacy, and the continuing significance of this thirteenth-century mystic in the twenty-first century. Including new translations of over 50 poems, each with extensive commentary, along with maps, a family tree, notes and a complete list of references, this is an essential introduction to Rumi, today's bestselling poet in the United States.

'This book is a major contribution to the study of the great Sufi poet, and it should be on the bookshelf of anyone drawn to Rumi.'

—*New York Review of Books*

'Terrific. Solid scholarship, combined with an articulate and highly readable style, will make this book accessible not merely to specialists but to the general reading public.'

—Dr Julie Meisami, Oriental Studies Institute,
University of Oxford

Franklin D. Lewis is Associate Professor of Persian Language and Literature at the University of Chicago. He is also the editor and translator of *Rumi: Swallowing the Sun*.

Paperback • 720pp • £19.99/$29.95 • 978–1–85168–549–3

RUMI: A SPIRITUAL TREASURY
Compiled by JULIET MABEY

Recognized as the world's greatest mystical poet, Rumi's ability to convey the very essence of the religious experience, to see the divine within the everyday, and to intoxicate the reader with his own passion lends his poems a universal quality. They have inspired generations of spiritual seekers, their timeless appeal speaking to all who walk the spiritual path of love.

This spiritual treasury offers selections drawn from Rumi's most famous poems and prose, arranged under a spectrum of headings exploring the spiritual life, from "The Sufi Way" and "Purifying the Heart" to "Living in the Spirit".

Complete with a helpful introduction to Rumi's life and work, and the ideals and practices of Sufism, this vibrant new anthology will be treasured by all, whether they seek enlightenment or simply a taste of some of the most profound literature ever written.

> Know that the outward form passes away,
> But the world of reality remains for ever.
> How long will you play at loving the shape of the jug?
> Leave the jug; go, seek the water!
>
> *Masnavi* II: 1020–1

"For anyone who seeks profound spiritual understanding, this has to be the introduction to buy. As an introduction to Rumi's work this book cannot be bettered. It distils the essence of his wisdom. It looks good, it feels good and it does your heart good. This *Spiritual Treasury* is an undoubted treasure in itself."

—Amar Hegedus, Chaplaincy Imam to the South London and
Maudsley NHS Trust, and co-author of
Sources of Islamic Spirituality

Paperback • 160pp • £9.99/US $14.95 • 978–1–85168–569–1

A RUMI ANTHOLOGY
Translated by REYNOLD A. NICHOLSON

This unique anthology combines two of the most famous books edited and translated by the great Victorian Persian scholar Reynold Nicholson, *Rumi: Poet and Mystic* and *Tales of Mystic Meaning*.

In *Tales of Mystic Meaning*, Nicholson has selected the most important stories and parables from the *Masnavi*, Rumi's famous thirteenth-century mystical poem, often described as the Bible of the Sufis. Professor Nicholson's elegant translations preserve the direct, semi-colloquial style of the tales, their lively dialogue, and the humorous depictions of human foibles so beloved of *Masnavi* fans.

Rumi: Poet and Mystic consists of an inspiring collection of over 100 delicately rhythmical mystical poems from Rumi's greatest works, exploring the profound themes of the nature of truth, of beauty, and of our spiritual relationship with God, together with brief explanatory notes.

Together, these classic texts from one of the most accomplished Rumi translators of all time comprise Rumi's best loved poems and stories, to bring a fresh accessibility to the great poet's work.

Reynold A. Nicholson was Sir Thomas Adams Professor of Arabic at the University of Cambridge, and a distinguished editor and translator.

Paperback • 384pp • £14.99/US $23.95 • 978–1–85168–251–5